# What Matters

## Reflections on Disability, Community and Love

Janice Fialka

Library and Archives Canada Cataloguing in Publication

Fialka, Janice, author
What matters: reflections on disability, community and love / Janice Fialka. -- [Updated and expanded edition]

Includes bibliographical references and index.
ISBN 978-1-987935-10-3 (paperback)
ISBN 978-1-987935-15-8 (ebook)

1. Children with disabilities--Family relationships. 2. Mothers of children with disabilities. I. Title.

HQ773.6.F52 2016 306.87 C2016-900791-X

First Edition - 1997 A Janice Fialka publication



Printed in Canada by Couto Printing & Publishing

**INCLUSION PRESS**

47 Indian Trail, Toronto
Ontario Canada M6R 1Z8
p. 416.658.5363 f. 416.658.5067
inclusionpress@inclusion.com

**inclusion.com** BOOKS • WORKSHOPS • MEDIA • RESOURCES

*To my parents, who taught me to dance to all life's music*

*To my children, Micah and Emma, who keep me dancing*

*To my husband, Rich — my dance partner*

• • • • •

*To those who remain with us in memory and spirit. You have shown us how to live with passion, purpose, perseverance, and pride. Your lives carry on through the stories we share.*

*Katie Beckett, Adam Michael Bertaina, Ryan Scott Colburn, Scott Christianson, Justin Dart, Matthew James Dolmage, James Weldon Ecford, Tracy Latimore, Laura Lee, David Kyle Ouellette, Alexis Mary Palmiere, Ed Roberts, Mayer Shevin, Loren Siegel, Robin M. Smith, Judith Snow, Jordan Ross Strickland, Charlie Swenson, Marlin D. Thomas, Jay Turnbull, and those whose names are not written here but live fully in our hearts.*

For additional copies of this book,
***www.inclusion.com***
or
Janice Fialka
10474 LaSalle
Huntington Woods, MI 48070
www.danceofpartnership.com

# TABLE OF CONTENTS

*Micah Fialka-Feldman*

# Foreword

I was 9 years old and my brother Micah was 13 years old when my mother first published *It Matters: Lessons from My Son.* I would often joke (although with some honest envious truth), "What about *Lessons from My Daughter?* I matter too!"

It was 1997. Inclusion was emerging as the way to provide opportunities for all students to learn. The Amendments to the Individuals with Disabilities Education Act (IDEA), signed during this year, reinforced the education of children with disabilities with their nondisabled peers and the importance of setting high expectations for students with disabilities. The historic civil rights legislation guaranteeing protection for people with disabilities, the Americans with Disabilities Act (ADA) of 1990, was just seven years old. Disabilities Studies had recently emerged as a course of academic study at Syracuse University in 1994. As our country's understanding of disability has evolved, so has our family's.

*Jerome Magid- photo*

In this updated and expanded edition (*What Matters: Reflections on Disability, Community and Love)*, you will bear witness to the continued journey of our family and glimpse the journeys of other families. There is no one way to live lives of dignity, determination, dreams, and dance. I know that

Micah is who he is because of a continued belief that risk-taking and building community are values that guide us.

*Micah with Yoshiko Dart*

In 2013, Micah spoke at the White House's 50th Anniversary of the Developmental Disabilities Assistance and Bill of Rights Act event. To honor the 25th Anniversary of the Americans with Disabilities Act (ADA) in 2015, my parents traveled to several cities with the huge hero puppet of Justin Dart, the father of the ADA, participating in marches and public events (http://www.adalegacy.com/ada25/ada-legacy-tour). Micah now works as a teaching assistant in the School of Education at Syracuse University. Much has changed since 1997.

I am now an elementary school teacher, teaching students with and without disabilities in my inclusive classroom. This is not easy work. Inclusion is still a practice and philosophy that families must fight for; it is not yet the expectation at schools and within communities. Recently, I had a second-grade student, Kevauna, with Down syndrome. Her family, not unlike my own, moved her from a substantially separate classroom in school to an inclusive setting. They, rightfully so, wanted Kevauna, their daughter and niece, to grow and thrive with her peers in an academically and socially rich environment. They have seen the stories of young

*Emma Fialka-Feldman (right) with her student Kevauna (center) and her mother Tamika (left)*

adults with intellectual disabilities attending universities; they are beginning to see how high expectations and imagination are part of the conditions necessary to her growth.

As I worked with Kevauna and her family, I took on another identity. I was no longer only the sibling of a brother with an intellectual disability and an advocate for disability justice. I was also a classroom teacher learning about how to make inclusion work. I found ways to meld disability history into my classroom teaching so that my students learned why all children belong in our classroom community. I discovered how many adults are needed to make inclusion work so that children grow socially and academically. I researched reading and math programs so that Kevauna, like her peers, could see herself as a mathematician, a reader, and a writer. I began to deepen my understanding about the other roles in my own brother's journey – the roles of teachers, self-advocates, families, and other service providers.

I have sat with families as they have received the news of their child's label and heard the reading of results from an IQ test. I have nudged and, at times, lovingly pushed families to be fiercer advocates for their children. I have reminded families to pay attention to the unique needs of the other children in their family – those without disabilities. I have connected families with resources that help families see the possibilities for their young child with a disability. This new edition, *What Matters: Reflections on Disability, Community and Love,* continues to be a book that surpasses time.

The stories, poems, and articles enclosed remind us that this work – for parents, family members, siblings, and professionals – is emotional, personal, and probably too often, overwhelmingly challenging. I share these stories with the families and educators with whom I work. May these poems and stories continue to spark discussion, raise expectations of possibilities, and validate emotions.

You are not alone – even if you feel like it. Whatever your

role, you are part of a journey of helping to create a world that works for many with dignity, determination, and dance – for families, for educators, and for individuals with disabilities. This book is no longer a story about Micah, "the son." *What Matters* now tells the stories of many people in many situations. These are honest stories written about and by Micah, stories about the roles of family members, and stories about the roles of professionals. *What Matters* is about giving dignity and voice to all who have chosen this journey, educators who have sought out this journey, and family members who were born into this remarkable journey. However we come to be on this journey, these articulations give voice to what matters.

Emma Fialka-Feldman
January 2016
http://emmaff.blogspot.com/

## PREFACE (2016)

It's been almost twenty years (and 9,000 copies) since this little book, *It Matters: Lessons from My Son*, was first published in 1997. I had no intention of writing a book at the time. I was raising two children, directing a teen health center, and speaking on the topics of parenting a child with disabilities and building parent-professional partnerships. It was my husband Rich Feldman who encouraged me – okay, strongly nudged me again and again! – to compile some of the poems and essays scattered across my messy desk into a booklet. He felt that a written component would be an important addition to my work and presentations. Although I initially resisted the idea, he turned out to be right. This collection has "mattered" so much to my journey as a mother, as a social worker, and most importantly as a person finding her way in this gloriously complicated world. The book has sparked others to share their stories of struggle, courage, and hope with me. Countless times it was their stories that sustained me and inspired my next step forward.

A year ago, Rich began persuading me again, this time to expand the book to include newer stories of Micah's journey into high school, college, work, and community living, as well as our family's journey of transformation through the decades. As before, I resisted and resisted until . . . well, here it is.

The new edition with its new title, *What Matters: Reflections on Disability, Community and Love* includes my writings from the 1997 edition, several of my newer published poems and essays, as well as new articles I have written especially for this new edition. I am honored to also include writings by my husband, Rich, our children, Micah and Emma, several interviews, and new articles by several important people from Micah's community in Detroit and Syracuse specifically written for this new edition. My hope is that the book captures how my understanding of what really matters to Micah, our family, and the community at large has deepened.

Micah has consistently shown us what matters to him, beginning early on when he announced (demanded!) in first grade that he no longer wanted to enter his school through a separate door into a self-contained classroom. "I want to go in the same door as all my friends" became our family's North Star. Micah realized his dream to be fully included in K-12 school, with supports. He insisted on being part of the wave of students with intellectual disabilities continuing their education, inclusively, on a college campus. He fought to live in the university dorm, which required a federal lawsuit. He eventually moved to Syracuse, New York – a seven-hour drive from our home – and is now a teaching assistant in the School of Education at Syracuse University. He lives in an apartment with a friend and has community support and a strong circle of friends. He speaks nationally and was recently appointed to the U.S. Presidential Committee for People with Intellectual Disabilities. His life is full. Each of those life events are wonderful for him and for those who he touches. Each has been possible because of Micah's determination, use of technology, enormously rich opportunities, and imaginative supports from others in his life!

When we ask Micah what really matters to him, he tells us it is having his voice and dreams respected and encouraged. What matters to him is the opportunity to belong and contribute in a variety of communities, to try things out, and to have cable TV!

Micah has deepened my understanding of the absolute brilliance of asking for help. He is at ease with what he can do and what supports he needs.

I love telling the story about one of Micah's first trips traveling by himself (another mother breathless moment!). He was not able to get a direct flight to his destination and thus had to change planes and gates at Chicago's O'Hare Airport – on his own. Micah has hundreds of sight words, but reading complicated signs is not part of his repertoire. With bated breath I waited for a reassuring phone call telling me he had arrived safely to the second gate. Finally, the call came and my breathing resumed! When I asked how he got from one gate to another, in different terminals, his response, tinged with annoyance was, "Mom, I just asked someone for help."

"Of course, Micah! Of course!" Once again he reminded me of how much time I waste "trying not to ask for help!"

The stories behind Micah's hard work and the vital support of his ever-expanding circle of friends are shared in this book, accompanied by the lessons I am still learning along the way.

I am excited to share our daughter Emma's insightful essays in this new edition. As you will observe, she writes with clarity and humor of her varied experiences – as our daughter, as Micah's sister, and now as a dedicated elementary teacher in an inclusive setting. Her stories deeply matter to us and to the many families, professionals, and students who have been touched by her honest, wise, and instructive words and teaching. She has deepened our understanding of parenting, disability, and humanity. I marvel at her ability to dance with both compassion for others and her strong conviction to demand high expectations for her students, her parents, and her brother. From an early age, she expanded our family's understanding of what mattered to her and ultimately to our family. She noticed when we, as parents, weren't being fair, firmly pointing out to us, "Hey, Micah CAN empty the dishwasher. We BOTH should have chores." She pushed Micah, in a way that only a sibling can, to try new things like learning to tie his shoes or paying the tip at restaurants. Just when we think we've figured out a way to support Micah or to grasp the complexity of a situation, Emma opens doors that we didn't even know existed.

And she makes us laugh out loud, just when we need it! Emma has become one of my best professors and mentors. I can't imagine my life without her "unpacking" of ideas, her diligent questioning, and her "love you mom" in my life.

For me, this collection of essays, articles, and poems is also another step in my own personal journey that began in a loving family in Flint, Michigan, in the 1950s. As a child, the values of caring for others and being curious and compassionate were strongly instilled in me by both my parents, especially my mother, who as a nurse worked with families with disabilities. Her storytelling at our kitchen table always communicated respect and high expectations for the children and families she met. Later in college in the late 1960s and 70s, I was fortunate to be active in the peace movement and the women's movement. From both movements, I learned the power of bold advocacy, the necessity of community, the insistence on justice for all, and the belief that the "personal is political." I took to heart the words of poet Marge Piercy whose poem "To Be of Use" was a guiding prayer for me. I fell in love with my husband for many reasons, certainly his sense of humor, and also because he is driven to make this world a better place. He is committed to visionary organizing and since the 60s has never lost his passion or purpose.

My professional training and work as a social worker reinforced my belief that building and sustaining relationships and making critical connections are the most important aspects of all work. I grew to understand that feelings, the messy ones, the piercing ones, the "facedown on the floor" ones, and the joyful ones are fundamental to our humanity and deserve our close attention and our validation.

I also realize daily how hard it is to truly listen, to truly be present with the other. I cling to the sage advice of Jane Wagner, who said, "Listen with an intensity that most people save for talking."

My struggles with uncertainty, self-doubt, and vulnerability knock me down often, but on my good days, I have learned to see them as windows to others who experience the same "knocking down" moments.

After 30 years as a mother and an even longer time as a social worker and human being, I am getting closer to a more enlightened understanding of what really matters. While Micah's accomplishments may appear tall in the stories, he and the disability community in particular have patiently taught me the true meaning of triumphs.

What matters is advocating relentlessly for what we believe in. It's listening to our children's dreams and keeping the conversation going as they change and evolve. It's seeking the support of others and offering support when needed. It's forgiving ourselves for pushing too hard – or not hard enough. It's about presuming possibilities and taking risks (even when it keeps us up at night). It's about having massive patience. It's redefining disability, not as a deficiency but as a difference, a natural part of the human condition, an imaginative way to live. It's redefining success and expanding our understanding of what it means to be human and proud.

As Micah taught me in the "airport story," what matters is

getting from one scary, unfamiliar gate to the next – not alone, but with others nearby. It's about knowing that there is not one way to live, walk, roll, see, move, hear, do, and be. It's about having the opportunity to fly – in an airport or toward our dreams – dreams that matter.

Janice Fialka
March 2016

*Unless otherwise credited, essays, articles, and poems without bylines were written by me.*

## PREFACE (1997)

One night in 1988, unable to sleep, I took my familiar yellow pad of paper, huddled in the corner of the couch, and wrote. I had a lot to say. Earlier that day my husband Rich and I had participated in a difficult meeting about our four-year-old son, Micah. His neurologist, occupational and physical therapists, speech therapist and others had sat with us at an immense wooden table, the kind I imagined King Arthur and his soldiers would have gathered around.

We all had known Micah's development was delayed, but at this meeting Rich and I formally learned that this was more than a temporary condition. His disabilities were significant and permanent. We left the meeting, descended the clinic stairs, walked to our car, and sobbed.

Although my cascade of tears had slowed late that night, I had a million rushing thoughts and feelings. It was soothing for me to pull the words out of my head and push them onto the yellow paper. That night I wrote "Advice to Professionals Who Must Conference Cases," one of the poems included in this booklet. The poem tells about my desire to have the well-intentioned professionals who were in attendance at this meeting do more than give a well-formulated clinical report. I needed them to be with me as a mother who was scared and grieving.

This one poem has opened many doors for me. It has traveled across the continent through newsletters, professional journals, textbooks. But most importantly its journey has been person-to-person. As a result of this poem I have had the good fortune to talk with deeply caring parents and professionals who have moved me through their stories of courage and compassion.

The first two poems in this booklet, "It Matters" and "For Pam," tell pieces of the stories of two strong mothers who fought hard to ensure that their children received what they needed.

"You Can Make A Difference in Our Lives" and "Feelings: The 'F-Word' in Parent-Professional Partnerships" both offer insights and suggestions to professionals who work with families and their children with disabilities. My parent voice is prominent in these two articles. I also draw on my personal experience as a veteran social worker of twenty years. Being Micah's mom has helped me to be a more sensitive social worker, especially to the subtle aspects of life-changing news. I have tried to weave both voices into these articles.

"A Hero's Poem: For Those Giving Life-Changing News" is a small tribute to the many professionals—educators, therapists, consultants, psychologists, physicians, and so on—who have fallen in love with Micah and other children like him, and who have worked tirelessly to create opportunities so all children can reach their potential. We need to say "thank you" more often to these dedicated people.

I have also included a journal entry about my experience as Emma's mother. Emma is Micah's younger sister by four years. She has brought balance and joy to our family. She astonishes us daily with her insights and wit. "*When a Sibling Asks the Tough Questions*" describes how I handled her first direct inquiry about Micah's differences.

The final poem, "The Gift of Support Groups," was literally written while driving home from a support group for parents of children with disabilities. I was bursting with energy as I felt the connection with people who understood me completely—who had "been there, done that" and who were helping me bolster my inner strength.

Just before taking this booklet to the printer I asked a new friend and colleague, Ann Herrold, to read my selections. I asked her for honest feedback. We hadn't shared many details about our lives, but I felt a sense of trust in her. As anticipated, she gave me excellent suggestions. Then she offered her story, "Chucky," about her 40-year-old brother-in-law who is developmentally disabled. When my husband and I read her story we sobbed—again! I knew that she had given me the perfect ending for this booklet. Hers is a story of love and hope.

I am blessed to be Micah and Emma's mom. Because of them and my husband, I am learning to live my own story of love and hope.

Janice Fialka
October 1997

# GRATITUDES

I could fill the pages of another book with the names of people who have supported me and my family over the years. My gratitude is deep, wide, and forever.

In the 1979 edition of *It Matters: Lessons from My Son,* I thanked and continue to thank Jan Adler, Alice Audie-Figueroa, Mimi Becigneul, Rita Benn, Kristen Birkmeier, Jan Boyd, Nancy Divinere, Al Frank, Sharyn Finkelberg, Joan Israel, Pat Linkhorn, Judy Lipshutz, Sharon McClinton, Carolyn McPherson (and her mighty green pen), Karen Mikus, Pam Mish, Val Overholt, Donna Sprague, Niquel Thurber, Ann and Rud Turnbull, and Kathy Williams.

At the core of my life is family, both Rich's ever-growing East Coast family and mine, especially my parents, my siblings, Gerry, Nancy, John, their spouses, and my nieces and nephews. I am blessed with a caring family who are there for the walks, talks, celebrations, bar and bas mitzvahs, and just when we need them.

Since the first publication in 1997, our family's village has grown exponentially. I am fortunate to have many "angels of the get-through" (an expression borrowed from the spoken word poet, Andrea Gibson) who do get me through the long nights, stuck sentences, and the swirling worries of the unknown. I regret if I neglected to include the names of important people who have supported me in meaningful ways. It is only because of my faulty aging neurons, not because I didn't notice your care.

My most sincere respect and gratitude extends to Sharon Berke, my Busy Women Reading Group, Kelly Boyle, James and Grace Lee Boggs Center, Ellen Bates Brackett, Leah Brock, Mary Jane Brotherson, B. Kay Campbell, Shirley Chalmers, Jennifer Champagne, Mel Clayton, Yoshiko Dart, Amy Dwyre D'Agati, Penny Hackett Evans, Cherie Fila, Lori Fithian, Michelle Friesen, my Gaia Group, Susan Boyer Gallagher, Jane Goldsmith, Meg Grigal, Dan Habib, Kae Halonen, Deb Hart,

Lisa Houghtelin, Shea Howell, Susannah Joyce, Lynda Kahn, Norm Kunc, Karen and Jeff Leitson, Sharon Lewis, Cindi May, Meg McSweeney, Michigan's Early On community, Michigan Roundtable for Diversity and Inclusion, Martha Mock, Rosa Naparstek, Shaun and Wes Nethercott, Naomi Ortiz, Michael Peterson, Amber Porter, Julia Putnam, Holly Sasso, Kim Sherobbi, Marlyn Shervill, Carolyn Sinai, Judith Snow, Sara Triano, Beth Swedeen, Emma Van der Klift, Dan Wilkins, Workmen's Circle and the disability justice community. Each person or group has contributed to my life in unique ways, and in ways that matter to me.

Micah's community in Syracuse has taught me and many others what interdependency looks like. Over the past few years the circle has included ARISE, Sarah Akin, Christy Ashby, Bud Buckhout, Thomas Bull, Caitlin Caron, Julie Causton, Lisa Coggi, Nikki Conroy, Michelle Damiani, Chelsy Daz, Kellyanne Doherty, Brent Elder, Jordan Feldman, Patricia Fratangelo, Rebecca Garden, Colleen Gibbons, Karly Grifasi, Wendy Harbour, Hillel, Betty Jones, Dee Katovitch, Katherine McDonald, Beth Myers, Kristine O'Brien, Onondago Community Living, Sarah Perry, Samuel Roux, Jennifer Russo, Mara Sapon-Shevin, Barbara Schloss, Steven James Singer, Karl Sterling, Andrea Stoughtenger, Alexander William Umstead, Katherine Vroman, Pam Walker, Heather Waters, Casey Woodfield, Eddie Zaremba and others whose names I might not know but whose friendship has made a difference.

In the final month of the manuscript, I owe enormous gratitude to Georgi Bargamian who spent countless hours on every word, comma, and period, bringing both her skill and full heart to her review. Kathy Garrett and Kathy O'Gorman leaped into action at the last moment with much needed and appreciated help with editing. Barbara Barefield created a delightful cover design. I am honored to have her creativity bookend our stories. Thank you to John Fox who carefully guided me to see what else needed to be said. During the final week, Jean Richardson leant me her mountain view, friendship, and computer. Thank you to Jean for introducing me to the wonderful Families of TIP at the Kirkridge Retreat and Study Center. (www.kirkridge.org)

Cathy Hollands' supportive feedback about the first edition of the book and her call-out for "more copies soon" began the process of thinking about a new edition.

A gargantuan thank you to Jack Pearpoint of Inclusion Press for enthusiastically saying, "Let's make the book." Jack's perseverance, deep understanding of "what matters," driving commitment to social justice, and exceptional skills at publishing, pushed this book into being. This new edition would not have happened without Jack. I am in awe of his commitment to his principles and practice.

My husband, Rich and our children, Micah and Emma "matter" to me more than I can ever describe. It is my privilege to dance through life with each of you. I laugh more, learn more, and greatly appreciate having an audience who allows me to read poetry to them at the kitchen table!

# Why This Book:
# Publisher's Introduction

It's Micah's fault. This book really began about three years ago when Micah phoned from Syracuse University where he was a teaching assistant. "It's time for another MAP.* When can you come?" That was the gist of that conversation and a relentless barrage of calls and emails from Micah proposing that we "do his MAP". Marsha and I had "done a MAP" with Micah many years before, and Micah decided it was time to do it again.

Our enthusiasm was comprehensive, but so was our schedule. We suggested options and attempted resistance. Resistance is futile with Micah. He persisted. Given his timetable, what he was asking (gently, beautifully and relentlessly) turned out to be the day before we were already booked to leave for work in Australia. For Micah, we drove to Syracuse, had another spectacular Micah experience thinking about his life and future, drove back to Toronto and boarded the plane for Australia.

Micah is a young friend and a great teacher. We learn a lot from Micah, and so can the world, which is why this book reinvented itself. We have become friends with Micah's parents, Janice and Rich, and Micah's sister Emma. As Inclusion Press, we had carried a wonderful little book written by Janice, "It Matters." But it was out of print. Unlike Micah, Janice shyly asked if we would consider reprinting the book. I was an enthusiast, and so the book began. Janice inquired with reticence, "Would it be okay to add a little more?" I was an enthusiast. Conversations continued, more and more articles were added, and now you have *What Matters*.

**Why is Inclusion Press so enthusiastic?**

- In part, Cathy Hollands, our Managing Director, talks to families as they order books. She reports, "It Matters" has had a profound impact on many families so we felt it must continue to be available as a resource for families.

** A MAP is a Person-Centered Planning approach developed by John O'Brien, Marsha Forest and Jack Pearpoint*

- This book is about relationships; everything is about relationships. That is the foundation. This book makes that simple truth crystal clear. We have a relationship with Micah and his family so the book fits our priorities.

- This book is an inspirational success story, and we all need to hear possibility stories. But Janice and family have the courage and humility to tell it all - gently and relentlessly. It was never easy. Many would say "but Micah is special - different - unique." That is true - but it is true for every human being - without exception. The gift in this book is telling the truth about this remarkable journey including relentless bumps and grinds, courage and endless love. That story is not about "success" in the "triumph" sense, but rather the accomplishment and contribution that any and every individual can make when people who love them are supported to identify and nurture the gifts of that person. Micah's story is remarkable and unremarkable. The "uber-success" is that through the love of his family, friends and supporters have found the essence of Micah, supported it enormously, and now we all reap the benefits.

- In this book, there are many important lessons articulated with love. One that speaks to me personally is a small explanation of how Micah writes. The answer is simplicity itself. He talks into his phone, and his phone 'transcribes' his thoughts and words into text. He doesn't "write" the words physically; he dictates them. So Micah's writing here is indeed Micah, speaking with his own remarkable eloquence. This "incidental" fact, is one of the many "helps" that could liberate the talents and creativity of millions of people around the world if they knew. And once they see the possibility, it is "self evident". Micah creates a window into that possibility.

Enjoy this wonderful book. It is a privilege to publish yet another wise contribution from our friends, Janice, Rich, Emma and of course, Micah.

Jack Pearpoint<br>
Inclusion Press<br>
June 2016

*Photos by Jerome Magid*

# *Early Years*

## It Matters

*(for a mother in Iowa)*

They say my two year old
can't see
can't hear
can't think

So why
send her to pre-school?

I say
because
just because.

They say
children like her
never go to school

They need
oxygen,
tubes,
hospital beds,
special care

So WHY
send her to pre-school?

I say
just because.

They say . . .
and on and on
and on, they say.

I'm persistent.
I say

because
because
because.
Then one day
my lioness
"BECAUSE"
wins.

My deaf, blind,
fragile daughter
goes to school.

She has
a teacher
a desk
a book.

At recess
butterscotch sunrays
warm her cheeks
and children's giggles
find paths to her heart.

For six glorious days,
she is finally
a student.
And I am finally a mother.

Nothing can take that from her
not even her
premature death
six days later.

She was and will always
be
my pre-schooler

just because.

## For Pam

Rural mother
snatched out of
quiet country.
Plopped rudely into
dense city traffic
and heat.

Soft, silky skin
paled.

Darkness crept into eyes and soul.

Too much noise,
Too many rushing faces,
Too many tubes
hooking her new born baby
to something
they called "life."

Waiting, waiting.
Walking down sterile corridors
Looking in
the eyes of doctors
for answers.

Not knowing the questions.
Only knowing
the lump in the throat.

More surgery.
More unknowns,
unknowns
unknowns
un knowns

Un knowing the world
that once was.

Then the
doctor raises his pitchfork of predictions
plunges the sharp points
into the mother's heart
and says:
"NOTHING LEFT, BUT TO
PUT THE BABY IN AN INSTITUTION."

Years later,
this baby, Andy
Learns to pick dandelions
with his new friend.
They giggle as their tiny fingers
pull each strand of yellow sunshine.

Mother smiles.

Oddly,
she remembers the doctor
and the pitchfork
that maimed her heart.

She whispers to the doctor:

"You could have told me with your heart.
You did not need to use your weapon."

She vows never to let another
pitchfork plunge
deep into the heart
of a grieving mother.

She thinks that she will
send a yellow dandelion
to this doctor.

She'll tell him that
Andy
picked it for him.

## You Can Make A Difference in Our Lives

*[Thoughts to professionals from a parent]*

I believe that as professionals who work with children with disabilities—educators, therapists, social workers, physicians, and so on—you can make a difference in our lives as parents of children with disabilities. You cannot, however, make THE difference. Therein lies the challenge of our partnership.

I want to highlight ten ways in which you can make an important difference.

**ONE: You have the opportunity not to be frightened by our anger . . . to embrace it, to welcome it, and even to invite it on a good day. Obviously, you cannot do it every day.**

You have the opportunity not to be intimidated when we blow off steam. You have the opportunity not to personalize these angry, negative feelings. The great challenge for you is to give us the opportunity to fall apart once in a while. You may be surprised by how quickly we recover when we are given the opportunity to feel our feelings in the company of experienced and caring professionals.

I have a tender spot in my heart for a particular physician who provided care for my son. Several years ago, my son was hospitalized with complications from a very serious seizure. My husband and I were scared and overwhelmed by all that we did not know or understand.

We were resting in the hallway of the hospital to get a break from the intensity of being with our child who was hooked up to numerous tubes. A group of physicians walked by, stopped at our son's doorway, and began to "conference the case." To my surprise I leaped from my chair and in a very loud voice lectured them on how this "patient" was MY son and a REAL human being.

The physician in charge was very kind and tolerant. He maintained eye contact with me, listened, acknowledged my fear, and then asked if he could accompany me to examine my son. I watched the other physicians in the group maintain their distance from me. However, this particular doctor remained engaged, responsive and accepting. Eventually, I used humor to discuss the particular event. His acceptance of my anger was almost as great a gift as his expert clinical care of my son. He had the great wisdom not to personalize the strong feelings. He understood their origin.

**TWO: You have the opportunity to decrease our profound sense of loneliness.** When my father was diagnosed with cancer several years ago, I was constantly approached by co-workers, friends, and neighbors, some of whom I hardly knew. With concern and kindness, they inquired about his health, his treatment and prognosis, and our family's adjustment. At the same time that I was dealing with my father's cancer, I was also dealing with my two-year-old who obviously had special neurological needs. I was baffled by the LACK of attention paid to the issue of my son. Very few people asked about my son's health, his treatment, his prognosis, or our adjustment. Society as a whole remains awkwardly silent about disabilities, especially cognitive disabilities. Very few people know what to say and thus feel unable to say anything.

Today you can buy a greeting card for many significant events, such as divorce, the death of a pet, an argument with your teenager, etc. There are, however, no cards dealing with our lives as parents of children with disabilities. Although it might be emotionally difficult to read such a card, in a way it also might help us feel "normal" and less alone. Something like: "Thinking of you as you learn your daughter is disabled" or "Give yourself a rest today from the hectic demands of speech, occupational, and physical therapy."

I am not suggesting that we create a new section of greeting cards! My point is that there is a blaring silence about our world. There are few opportunities to read or hear about our lives and the lives of our children. This awkward silence results in more silence, which intensifies our sense of loneliness.

You have the opportunity to break that silence and gently lead us into the sounds of compassion and respectful curiosity. So often we want to talk about "it" but few people appear to want us to talk. You often will be the ONE person who will say: *Tell me more. And then what happened? And how did that feel?*

**THREE: You have the opportunity to anticipate and normalize our feelings**. You can prepare us for the challenges of birthdays and holidays. You can let us know that we will have wild mood swings and uncomfortable thoughts about "those parents" with typical children.

I vividly recall one physical therapist hesitantly handing me an article which described some of my son's disabilities. She explained she had had the article for several months but was reluctant to share it with me because I might cry. At the time, I thanked her for the resource. However, what I wanted to do was scream, "Of course I'll cry. This is not fun. It's okay to cry. Part of your job is to help me to cry."

Never underestimate the significance of your anticipation and acceptance of our feelings. It will comfort us during those long sleepless nights.

**FOUR: You have the opportunity to help us re-enter the "world of normal families."** Parents never feel the same once they learn about their children's differences, especially when the differences are cognitive. We don't know how to squeeze back into the world despite the fact that we are in it. Going to a birthday party can be a major mountain to climb. You, as the professional, can create bridges back to that world.

I am reminded of the story of one family whose child had been in the Neonatal Intensive Care Unit (NICU) for several months. It was his time to be released from the hospital despite his ongoing special medical and developmental needs. The NICU nurse asked the parents to identify a few neighbors. She said she knew that it is often awkward for new parents to bring home a child with disabilities. Parents often do not know what to say to family and friends. The nurse indicated her interest and willingness to phone a few friends and family members to explain the situation and offer suggestions for assisting the family. The parents were overcome with gratitude.

Some professionals invite parents to bring a family member or friend to a therapy session. It is often easier for the professional to introduce the information and to model how to talk about these sensitive issues.

**FIVE: You have the opportunity to help us know our child.** In the beginning, most of us know very little about the disability. We often can't even spell this new reality of our lives. You can model for us how to say the words, how to tell others. You can take us into our children's lives.

I had lunch with a friend whose child is multiply impaired, including a visual impairment. She had been feeling very frustrated, in part because she did not understand her son's world. The therapist suggested that she apply Vaseline to her eyeglasses and experience her child's world for an hour. It worked! My friend was thrilled to see the world through her son's eyes. This therapist had simply shared her knowledge. To my friend she had been given a way to fall in love with her son once again.

**SIX: You have the opportunity to share books, pamphlets, and other resources.** Take those books and articles out of your file cabinets and off the shelves and share them with parents who have no idea where to find the stories and facts about their children. It is very challenging to walk to the "disability" section of a bookstore or library. You can bring it to us and even sit next to us as we tentatively open those pages.

**SEVEN: You have the opportunity to recognize and celebrate our victories.** They are often too small for the "normal" population to appreciate. You know that the awful sounding "grunt" made by our child is truly a miracle. Only you know that a new movement is significant and indicates a renewed sense of hope. You can point out these grand milestones to us.

**EIGHT: You have the opportunity to remind us how far we have come and how much we have accomplished.** You, often more than our closest friends, know the details of our successes. Over and over, you can highlight those changes and celebrate the growth.

**NINE: You have the opportunity to allow us those moments when our souls fall into deep despair.** We will at times feel that we cannot continue for another moment. We will at times feel that we don't want to continue for another moment.

You can give us the space to be in that dark place. It is one of the greatest "interventions" you can provide.

**TEN: If at times you can do some of these nine suggested activities, you will then have the opportunity to help us feel hope.** We must feel hope if we are to get to our next appointment, or to face the next birthday party, or to use the word "disability."

Effective partnerships between parents and professionals require collaboration. Plopped right in the middle of that word you will find the word *"labor."* Partnership is labor. It is hard work. You are the midwives helping us give birth to a new relationship. Let us begin.

*This article was originally published in the Early On Newsletter, Vol. 3, No. 4.*

# Advice to Professionals Who Must "Conference Cases"

Before the case conference,
I would look at my almost five-year-old son
And see a golden haired boy
Who giggled at his baby sister's attempts to clap her hands.
Who charmed adults by his spontaneous hugs and hellos.
Who captured his parents with his rapture with music and
his care for white-haired people who walked a walk
a bit slower than younger folks,
Who often became a legend in places visited because of his
exquisite ability to befriend a few special souls,
Who often wanted to play "peace marches,"
And who, at the age of four
went to the Detroit Public Library
requesting a book on Martin Luther King.

After the case conference
I looked at my almost five-year-old son.
He seemed to have lost his golden hair.
I saw only words plastered on his face.
Words that drowned us in fear.
Words like:
Primary expressive speech and language disorder
severe visual motor delay
sensory integration dysfunction
fine and gross motor delay
developmental dyspraxia and RITALIN now.

I want my son back. That's all.
I want him back now. Then I'll get on with my life.

If you could see the depth of this pain
If you could see the depth of our sadness
then you would be moved to return
our almost five-year-old son
who sparkles in the sunlight despite his faulty neurons.

Please give me back my son
undamaged and untouched by your labels, test results, descriptions and categories.

If you can't, if you truly cannot give us back our son
Then just be with us quietly, gently and compassionately as we feel.

Sit patiently and attentively as we grieve and feel powerless.
Sit with us and create a stillness
known only in small, empty chapels at sundown.
Be there with us
As our witness and as our friend.

Please do not give us advice, suggestions, comparisons or another appointment. (That's for later.)
We want only a quiet shoulder upon which to rest our too-heavy heads.

If you can't give us back our sweet dream
then comfort us through this evening.
Hold us. Rock us until morning light creeps in.
Then we will rise and begin the work of a new day.

You can hear Janice read this poem, accompanied by music and photos at: http://www.broadreachtraining.com/videos/advice.htm.

# Twenty-six years later: Reflections on *Advice to professionals who must 'Conference Cases'*

Twenty-six years ago, in the middle of a sleepless night, I put pen to paper and scribbled on my yellow legal pad "Advice to Professionals Who Must 'Case Conference'." Some now call it a poem. But at that unimaginable moment it was wild emotions rushing out while tears swiftly streaked down my cheeks. It hadn't been an easy meeting to sit through. The labels used about my almost five-year-old son felt like speeding bullets fired directly into the bull's eye of my mother-heart.

At this case conference, I wanted something from the professionals other than their careful assessments and necessary labels. I knew they cared. I could see it in their eyes and in the way they leaned forward, cleared their throats, and tried to soften their voices. But I wanted more from them---or something different than what felt like a firing of labels.

What was the "more" I wanted?

I have spent the last 26 years trying to define that "more."

In my conversations, research, writing, and training over the years, I think I now have a slightly better idea. I wanted to hear, through their words and gestures that they understood that this news was hard to hear. I wanted them to pause from their reports and just BE with me and my scattered feelings of being stunned, scared, vulnerable, and uncertain. I was swirling in so many conflicting emotions. Guilt, worry, deep love for my son, more worry, why me?, why this?, do I have what it takes?

I wanted my feelings acknowledged, responded to, validated or even just heard. At the time, I was too discombobulated to know exactly what I was going through . . . but I knew it was life-changing and I wasn't sure I could handle it.

I wanted them to mirror back to me what I was going through. I wanted an emotional connection---a heart-to-heart sense of being in the presence of someone who was a witness to my feelings. Not for the purpose of making it "all better" . . . or "fixing it" . . . but rather to be given the space to feel, to have the gift of validation for what seemed impossible to name.

I did NOT want pity or sympathy (I did not want any "poor Janice" thoughts).

I did want compassion and thoughtful acknowledgement. I wanted to feel that at least one of the professionals understood my feelings and could demonstrate in simple words that my feelings made sense. I wanted them to be comfortable with my immense uncomfortableness.

Over the years I have learned that this ability to identify, understand, respond and demonstrate compassion is a skill and --- more importantly, a way of being with someone. Perhaps it was basic empathy I wanted, not just well-crafted reports. I think what I was attempting to scribble on my yellow legal pad during that sleepless night was . . . don't rush me, don't overwhelm me with more data, just BE with me for a few precious moments. Be at ease with my uneasiness.

Sometimes I think professionals worry that if they respond to a family's feelings they won't have time to address pressing issues, discuss the goals and objectives, or deal with imposed requirements. I understand this worry. Professionals have many demands and are responsible for many lives. However, in most situations, a few moments of truly being present with the family, beyond the report-giving and data-sharing can enhance the sense of trust and comfort a family feels in meetings, and often leads to a better rapport. Putting aside the lengthy reports for a few moments and inviting families to share stories, sparked by conversational questions like, "What does your child enjoy doing? What is hard about your day at home? What do you want us to know about your child?" can soften the reoccurring stiffness present in many meetings.

How do professionals shift meetings from "stiff" to "more relaxed?" One way is to tune into and validate the feelings, both their own and those of the families. In most cases this attention to feelings doesn't require longer meetings. It does require "work of the heart" and a practiced-tolerance for uncertainty.

Many professionals have helped me understand that this "being with" families during highly emotional times isn't easy for them. It isn't that they don't care, but rather that they often don't have the comfort and confidence in handling uncomfortable or strong emotions. They may possess, what I call, inside empathy but lack the confidence or competence to demonstrate outside empathy.

Tender moments like the meeting I wrote about in this poem are challenging for everyone, not just for me. I have a better understanding of this now after more than three decades of being Micah's mom. I now appreciate that, if at those meetings, we are able to feel our shared humanity and our shared vulnerability, we have the potential to transform how we relate to each other, and to ourselves.

Perhaps this is what we call kindness. At the "best" meetings, we move ever so slightly out of the strict labels of "parent" and "professional" and into the shared label of "human being." In reality we are all trying our best, struggling to learn how to connect, wanting to be understood, not fixed, and longing to be validated and valued for our unique messiness and humanness.

## School Lessons

Excitement is high.

New clothes hang on the bodies of charged
little boys and girls.

The air is pierced by a mixture of reluctance and spirit.

I glance at familiar faces of neighborhood moms.
A few have taken me under their wing.
I want so much to feel their same pleasure.
It is their child's first day of the new school year.
I want to proudly walk to my son's new room.

I want to chat with moms and wonder
if their children will become my child's new friends.
I want to wonder what birthday invitations await my son.

I want to climb
that mountain staircase leading to the THIRD GRADE

I want to hold my son's hand
and enter the new room of his new grade.

I want that experience so much.
I would exchange almost anything for it.

But I cannot have it.

My child is kept
on the first floor
despite the rise of all the other nine year olds.

I enter his special education classroom.
I want the room to look like all other classrooms.
I want there to be parents talking
(but these children are bussed)
I want there to be children chasing each other.

It will not be that way.
So I take my cue from my son.
He is smiling.
I slap on a smile.

I wear that plastered smile down the hallway
past the beaming parents.
I walk alone.
Inside I ache for what seems so available to others.

It is my son's first day of third grade.
I'm not ready for this lesson.

# When a Sibling Asks the Tough Questions

*[At the age of 7, my daughter, Emma, asked me about her 11 year-old brother's differences. As parents we had always focused on our son Micah's strengths and abilities which were similar in many ways to his peers. As both Micah and Emma grew, his differences and her ability to see the differences increased. This journal entry captures the particular moment when Emma unexpectedly asked me "the tough question."]*

You, Emma, are becoming more aware of Micah and his differences. You are wanting me to know you know. I'm uncertain about what you know or how you know, but I listen intensely for cues which will reveal your creeping awareness.

A recent conversation started during your bedtime bath, "I'm just, well, Mom, I'm just asking if Micah always said ah-ah-ah." (referring to his dysfluency) "Did he do that when he was a baby, Mom?"

I strain to hold the features of my face ever so still. I do not want you to pick up any feelings from me. It is important to me that you experience total acceptance as you relate your observations about Micah to me.

"No, he didn't stutter as a baby. Stuttering is another word for ah-ah-ah. No, he didn't. That happened more recently. It started when he was 8 years old."

I search quickly for the right words and the right inflection to my voice. Rules flash across my brain like the multiplication flash cards I practiced as a child.

1. Answer questions directly.

2. Show no strong emotions.

3. Pause. Wait. Give time to hear her thought.

4. Remember that her questions are not burdened by the same reality as yours.

I continue. I surprise myself with my outer sense of comfort and confidence - not, however, matched by my inner worry.

I say, "Remember when we met Dr. Daly? He's a speech doctor and he's gonna help Micah with his stuttering." I watch you carefully as if I am watching a tiny ant climb across my index finger.

You begin to lose interest. I don't want to push, and yet a part of me finally wants to begin this conversation. Part of me wants to blurt out: "Yes, Micah has a disability. He is developmentally disabled. (I still can't use the m____________ r____________ words.) And he will always be that way."

But I didn't say that—not yet.

I take a deep breath. You continue. "Mom, Micah doesn't read. I read. It seems like I should be older than him." Then you immediately reassure yourself (or maybe me), "It's okay. Everyone is different. I just want to understand this."

I remember to breathe slowly—to take in the air and let it out lightly as if my lungs are tip-toeing to a lullaby. "You're right. Micah can only read a few words. You are reading many words."

And then I take the plunge. I know I must begin but part of me wants to stay in the old way of pretending that maybe you don't have to know. "Micah is in special education." I feel dizzy. Can I really be saying this now? Wait, I'm not ready. I haven't practiced exactly what I will say. And yet words are coming out of my mouth.

. . . and they even sound coherent.

"What's special education?" you inquire.

"Some people need special teachers to help them when they are having some problems with reading." I pause. I can tell you are interested. I continue. "You know how Grandma Dee uses a cane to help her walk?"

"Yes," you say knowingly. I can tell it feels familiar to you.

"Well, Micah needs some help with his reading, like Grandma needs some help with walking."

"Oh." And then off you chatter about less important things.

We did it, Emma. We had that first "real talk" during a quiet unplanned moment on the cold bathroom floor. You've probably been thinking about it for a while—not a lot, just once in a while. I've been thinking about it for a lifetime of eight years.

I leave the room feeling as if I might not be able to catch my breath and might not be able to hold back the flood of tears. But that's not all. I also am feeling an odd sense of peace. I did "it" today. You asked. I listened. I answered. You asked more. I responded more and for the moment you felt satisfied.

I think I'll probably look back on this baptism as an easy conversation compared to the more challenging ones that await us. I do know that first impressions are significant and I think this first conversation went fairly well. I'm proud of the preliminary work that I did in preparation for this first conversation and, interestingly, I am grateful to my mother for using a cane . . . at least for this tender moment. Once again, my mother was there to help me walk this journey. She "loaned" me her cane and I danced rather gracefully—using it to steady myself. Even when my mom is not with me, she has a way of being there in exactly the right way.

Grandma's cane was the bridge that brought familiarity and strength to something that felt odd and scary.

It was a good beginning, dear Emma.

## Two months later

*[This journal entry was made while vacationing as a family on Sutton Island off the coast of Maine. We went hiking together as a family.]*

It's lunch time and we've reached our destination. We've walked through the lush forests of this quiet island. We've taken in the sweet smells of pine cones and green moss. We now stand tall on the caramel-colored rocks which lunge into the jeweled ocean. I have instructed you two to find the "perfect rock place" to eat our simple lunch of peanut butter and jelly sandwiches.

Emma and Micah, you tentatively try out walking on these huge jagged rocks. Gradually you recognize that the rock edges form oddly-placed stair steps that lead from one end of the shore to the other. Up and down, over and across, your eyes carefully locate the flat surface which will snugly hold your small feet. Soon, Emma, you are ahead of Micah. Your unexpected joy at climbing rocks captures your spirit. You fly across the sharp edges of stone barely touching the hard surfaces. You look back at us and see your brother climbing, but at a slower pace. You instantly pause. You watch Micah carefully plan out his placement of foot, hand, and body And in complete honesty you call out to your brother, "You're a good rock climber, Micah."

And indeed he is, as evidenced by his perseverance and commitment to meet his sister at the "perfect picnic place." You, Emma, continue your climb with joyful vim and vigor, but this time you find a circuitous route which keeps you climbing, but not too far from your brother.

## The Label

The first label
plastered on my son's tiny forehead
was *jaundiced*.

"Don't worry" they said.
I wondered: "How do you do that?"

The second label
smeared on my son's perfect lips
was *failure to thrive.*

"It's not because you are a bad mother" they said.
I wondered: "Why do I feel like one?"

The next label
hammered on his head
was "He's-going-to-be-fine."
Oh, how I wanted to believe that one.
I tried.

That label was soon ripped away
only to be rudely replaced with:
neurologically impaired THEN
developmentally delayed THEN
yup-this-is-a-long-term-condition THEN
learning disabled THEN
seizure disorder THEN
educable mentally impaired THEN
trainable mentally impaired THEN

"Oh yes I've got it":
low-functioning-
educable-mentally-impaired-
with-learning-disabilities.

There is only one label remaining.

It is for the mother:

RAGING BULL

# A Hero's Poem:
## For Those Giving Life-Changing News to Families

*For Karen and other professionals who work*
*with parents of children with disabilities*

You have chosen
this work

You must deliver
the harsh words
to parents who pace in the middle of the dark night.

It is a hero's job
but doesn't feel like one

No one celebrates your achievements
or asks you,
under the bright lights of tv cameras:
"What does it feel like to be a hero?"

If they asked me—one of the parents who pace—
I'd tell them.

You forge into burning buildings
where scorching flames melt dreams
and noxious fumes choke back hope.

You extend your hand
pulling us out of the blazing heat
that consumes what we know and love.

You sit with us in smoke-filled rooms
that blind us from seeing the child we bore.

You search for gentler ways
to say the words that
singe our hearts

and you do this over and over and over.

Don't be afraid to touch your lips
with the same drops of cool water
you tenderly offer to us.
There will be more of us who need you, dear hero.

# Feelings: The "F-word" in Parent-Professional Partnerships

I was sitting in one of those meetings where everyone wished that they were someplace else. The fake smiles could not dissipate the thick fog of tension that impaired our vision. I, the parent of a child with disabilities, was being told that my son's dysfluency (I used to call it stuttering, but I've caught up with the jargon) had reached serious levels and needed immediate and intensive intervention. There had been some hints that this information was coming, but no amount of preview and practice ever adequately prepares me for the earthquake. It is only when the walls are shaking, the windows are shattering, and the dust from the plaster is blinding me, that I "get it" and then utter: "Oh, so this is what it means to have the earth split under your feet."

I knew the school professionals involved in this meeting cared about my son, but at the moment I did not feel their well-meaning intentions, especially after the speech therapist shook her finger in my husband's face to emphasize her point. My husband and I believed the recommended intervention was inappropriate and might lead to an awkward self-consciousness for my son. As far as we could tell, he did not appear even remotely aware of his dysfluency. Our fear was that if we drew his attention to what we were learning to call his "bumpy speech," it would result in even more bumps and bruises to his ego. We were worried about his dysfluency, but our gut told us that the proposed intervention was too much for him.

The upward curves to the glued-on smiles began to sag as the tension mounted. This, however, did not stop the team members from lecturing on their perspectives, even when no one was really listening. In my weak attempt to "stay cool" I allowed my eyes to wander around the classroom. I tried to distract myself from the tension by looking at the numerous posters and colorful items that decorate the walls of a school classroom. Ironically, my eyes rested on the poster that seems almost as common as the "ABC" posters. It is the one with the heading: "How are you feeling today?" Beneath the words are exaggerated pictures of a boy depicting such emotions as disgust (his tongue is hanging out), hysterical (his eyes are crossed, his hair is standing up, and his mouth open beyond ability), and enraged (teeth clenched, the beady eyes staring in a devilish gaze).

I glanced at each illustration and stopped on the faces that fit my feelings: angry, hysterical, frustrated, hurt, disgusted, frightened, enraged, depressed, overwhelmed, lonely (yes, lonely), surprised, anxious, and shocked. I reviewed them again and again. I found my body loosening just a bit. It helped me to acknowledge my intense feelings of the moment.

It's not easy for us to hear about our child's disabilities, especially if there is a long history of "bad news." Intellectually, we know we need to hear the information, but certainly it is not anything we look forward to. At each of those "bad news" meetings, our unruly feelings invade our bodies and stab our hearts. "Not again," we want to whine.

Reluctantly, I pulled my thoughts back to the meeting - the one at which no one wanted to be. The words of each team member flew around and around the table. It was then that I wanted to scream: "Feelings! Feelings! Can't you see them leaping all over the table? Will you please stop and acknowledge their presence? They are screaming at all of us for attention." But I did not cry out my insight. Instead I tried desperately to restrain those unruly visitors. They didn't obey. I felt them creeping into my rising voice, and tightening my facial movements and stiffening my neck. It was then that I reluctantly realized that feelings is the "F-word" in parent-professional partnerships. No one seemed to be prepared to deal with the strong emotions, so we didn't or we tried not to. We just pretended that "they" weren't there or that "they" would go away soon. Feelings seemed to be irrelevant and inappropriate to the content of this meeting. We wondered judgmentally: "What do feelings have to do with setting goals for the child and establishing interventions? Let's get on with the 'real work.'"

Guess what?

Sometimes the real work is dealing with feelings.

Despite the fact that our children are exposed to the "How are you feeling today?" poster, we as adults often fail miserably at paying attention to these thirty or more feelings. We still don't seem to "get it." We still don't "walk the talk" or "feel the feeling."

What would it be like if we were "good" at feelings? What would our team meetings be like? What would partners say or do if we stopped pretending that feelings were not present during our interactions? What would happen if we acknowledged that huge elephant in the room which everyone sees and no one speaks about?

## Guiding Principles for the "F-Word"

1) Teams of parents and professionals should initially set the norm that feelings, especially strong ones, are to be expected during meetings. Raising and educating children, especially children with disabilities, are among the most challenging adventures we adults face. If we are doing it well, both parents and professionals will experience strong emotional reactions: intense feelings of fear (yes, fear), investment, care, responsibility, concern, protection, and commitment.

2) Feelings are physiological reactions to incidents. They arise in part because of our values, our past experiences, and current expectations. Just as it is impossible to will away a high fever or a strong sneeze, we cannot will away feelings (Hall, 1995). Feelings need to be acknowledged and understood, not judged. Feelings are often confused with behavior. Feelings can influence behavior, but feelings are not actions. Only behavior is a result of a conscious and willful decision.

3) Feelings are not predicable nor do they follow rules of logic. Instead, emotional reactions sweep over parents unexpectedly. Triggers for such strong responses can be as simple as: a school display of children's art; the sight of a typically developing child at the school's entrance; planning for an in-school party; seeing one's child standing alone on the playground; or the off-handed use of a single word by a well-intentioned team member during a meeting. Suddenly, the feeling is there, unexpectedly, without an invitation.

4) Actual events and future possibilities mean different things to parents and professionals. Something a professional might celebrate might trigger sadness in a parent. I recall that at one of my son's concerts he was asked to be the flag-bearer during several of the patriotic songs. His face beamed with pride as he strained to hold up the pole. Periodically, one of his classmates quietly went to his side to help him re-position the drooping flag. At first my husband and I were pleased with the important role he played. We were happy he had a meaningful role in the concert and that he was feeling a warm sense of accomplishment.

Then—like a bolt of lightning—I was struck by all the moving mouths of all the fifth graders. They sang all the songs and read all the music. I was rudely reminded of Micah's limitations that prevented him from reading and remembering the words. There he stood, tall and proud but with closed mouth out of which no song flowed. I saw his differences, and I saw him standing apart from his peers.

Did my feelings of love and pride for my son vanish? Absolutely not. But other feelings of sadness, loss, and fear crept into the concert. I wondered if he would continue to find meaningful ways to participate. I wondered if his accepting peers of today would be as tolerant of him as they approached those difficult middle school years. My feelings and wonderings were uninvited, but ever so present.

It is usual for parents to anticipate future isolation or difficulty

as they see their child with disabilities function within a typical peer setting. What seems wonderful to a teacher may be bittersweet, even painful, for a parent.

I am appreciative when professionals are alert to the presence of my feelings and respond empathically.

5) Never underestimate the importance of validating feelings. Validation occurs when the feeling is named or acknowledged. *"This seems frustrating to you. Tell me more about that."* The spirit of the acknowledgment is one of respect and understanding. It may be useful to ask for elaboration or clarification of the feeling. *"How did you get to this feeling? Tell me a bit more about the worry."* There should be no judgment of the feeling, as in, *"You shouldn't feel angry; I was just trying to help."*

Validation of feelings is a powerful strategy because it sends the message that someone understands you and the feeling, at least for the moment. Validation does not imply agreement with the feeling. When you validate, you communicate that the feeling is genuine and understandable from a given perspective. Sometimes professionals seem to skip over a discussion or recognition of feelings, yet parents often report that they work best when professionals display compassion or support. Out-loud identification of feelings is one way to express compassion.

Referring to my earlier description of the meeting at which no one wanted to be present, it would be helpful if one of the professionals had acknowledged there was an obvious disagreement that needed more attention. During that meeting we had voiced our reluctance to accept the proposed treatment plan for our son's dysfluency. At that particular moment "selling" or telling us more about the proposed strategy was not useful, and only seemed to add to the polarization. We all, parents and professionals, needed a break or change from the current direction of the discussion. There was no acknowledgment of any feelings. We were pretending that we were engaged in a fruitful discussion when in fact no one was really listening to anyone. We were all preparing what to say next in order to convince each other of the correctness of our perspective.

It would have been beneficial if one of the professionals had offered some insight as in, *"It seems that we are at a standstill. Feelings are strong right now. As parents, what are you most worried about? Help us understand what troubles you about this plan."* Genuine inquiry and sensitivity to our worry would have allowed us as parents to voice and clarify our concerns and to feel the support of the professional.

It also would have been helpful for one of the team members to acknowledge our feelings as parents. We felt trapped, worried about our son, alone, fearful, and confused. At the same time it did not appear that anyone knew this or at least was willing to support us through these feelings. That all-too-familiar and troubling feeling of "us" and "them" grew to monster-like proportions.

A single but genuine recognition of our feelings would have engaged us and allowed us to re-enter that conversation.

6) Strong feelings that are not constructively dealt with through validation and empathy will interfere with productive problem-solving. As Buckman suggests (1995), unacknowledged feelings are like a piece of spinach caught in a person's front teeth. Until it's removed, distraction prevails and no clear thinking occurs.

7) Acknowledging feelings does not make them go away. Sometimes a brief mention of the feeling is all that's needed;

at other times, naming the feeling and talking a bit about it are important. Professionals can take their cues from the parent. It is useful to "listen" to a person's nonverbals as well as his or her words.

8) It is not helpful to ignore tears. It is normal and appropriate for a person to cry when sad. Pause, offer the person some tissue, and wait a bit. It may be appropriate to lean toward the person or to inquire, *"Can you tell me about the tears?"* The professional can normalize the emotions: *"This is hard stuff to experience. It is understandable that you'd cry or feel sad."*

9) De-personalize without minimizing a parent's feelings or the cause of the feelings. Even when you, as a professional, have made a mistake and truly are the source of the difficulty or pain, allowing yourself to feel personally attacked usually results in defensiveness. Instead, acknowledge the other person's feelings, apologize, and attack the mistake. If you are not the cause, you may still be the recipient of anger, distress, or anxiety because there are no other targets at the time for these difficult feelings. Again, listen closely and give the feelings a name. Caring inquiry may help both of you more fully understand the situation.

10) Professionals need support and training to recognize the importance of feelings and to gain comfort and skills in dealing with them effectively. Working in the field of special education or disabilities is rewarding. It is also strenuous. Ongoing supervision or consultation to process feelings, to share struggles, and to disclose discomforts are critical to maintaining the spirit "to go forward in this work."

## In conclusion

There are many reasons feelings are the "F-word" in forming partnerships between parents and professionals. Feelings frighten us. We feel inexperienced around them. Many of us have been the targets of undeserved displays of emotions. We have had little training in how to deal with them. We received strong messages as children about ways to handle and not handle feelings. Thus it makes sense that we often avoid them, deny them, or just ignore them.

But feelings can be our best friends. They let us know when something is brewing inside which needs attention or consideration. Strong feelings are often present when we care about someone or something.

Feelings can strengthen relationships. When we respond to someone's feelings of grief, anger, or fear with sensitivity, we create an opportunity to enhance the relationship. Think about a time when someone validated your strong feeling of sadness or joy. Their comment—their recognition—probably increased your sense of connection with that person. Feelings can lead us to insight and deeper understanding of what is really important.

By practicing the suggestions offered in this article, we can increase our ability to handle feelings in a constructive and careful manner. It is not enough to hang the poster "How are you feeling today?" in the classroom. If we want to be effective in our relationships, we need to take the question off the poster and use it in our conversations with ourselves and our partners. Maybe then we'll begin to realize that feelings do not have to be the "F-word."

## References

Hall, D. October, 1995. Workshop on partnerships. Presentation at the "Partners in Care" Early On Technical Assistance Conference, Ann Arbor, MI

Buckman, R. (1992). *How to break bad news: A guide for health care professionals.* The Johns Hopkins University Press, Baltimore.

*The author was partially supported by the W. K. Kellogg Foundation Grant #POO343324 in writing this essay.*

# The Gift of Support Groups

You are with me everywhere now.

At all the meetings, conferences, IFSPs and IEPs.
At each discussion I have, there you are
Lyn, Marilyn, Jan, Rick and especially Ronna.

I take you all with me.
I tuck you "as a group" into my pocket
when I have to face all those professionals
who can't make my child normal.
While in my pocket, I hold on to you tightly,
And you, my wonderful friends, hold on tightly to me.

When they, with a capital "T" unintentionally say something
that scorches my soul,
You "as a group" gather around my hand-in-pocket.
You sing to me.
You tell me to hang on.
You comfort me.

You are my adult elves that I can take anywhere and always.
I can carry on
because you are with me.

It's like this . . .
I don't feel as alone anymore.

Yes, yes, of course I must walk this journey by myself.
But—from now and forever
when I need it most
You are there in a way that makes a difference.
When I say it is hell,
You know what I mean.

When I say I am enraged,
You know what I mean.
When I say it is unrelenting
and hurts more than I ever knew pain could hurt,
You believe me.

You nod
        and I know I've been heard.
So, dear elves
Come with me.
And when it's not my turn to fight another battle.

I'll leap into your pockets
and hold onto your hands.

# Chucky's Story

*By Ann Herrold*

When I was in elementary school I lived across the street from a family with six kids. They had toys and "stuff" everywhere. They seemed different than the other families.

The key to the whole thing was that their fourth kid was a "retard." His name was Chucky. He was labeled "borderline trainable." The professionals told his parents he wouldn't live very long, had epilepsy, and that they should put him in an institution. But his parents wouldn't do that. They just stuck him in the middle of their family and acted like everything was normal.

We could tell when Chucky was coming down the street because he walked like a drunk. He looked kind of goofy and gave the whole family a less-than-perfect image. Chucky got lost; we all searched for him. Chucky fell down; we all picked him up. Chucky got teased; we all stood up for him.

We didn't know it then, but Chucky gave us all a common cause. He was not only a part of his family, but a part of us, too. He re-defined "retard" for us and made us compassionate for other humans. And we re-defined Chucky. This "borderline-trainable" kid went to elementary, junior high and high school. He took cooking classes and was the manager of the varsity football team. He went on family vacations, met the governor, and learned, with the help of his family and community, to live in the world.

In 1977 I married Chucky's brother. Chucky couldn't come to the wedding because he was in Colorado competing in the Special Olympics! So now that less-than-perfect family that has a retarded kid was MY FAMILY! How could that happen? How could I CHOOSE to be a part of that? Well, here's how: while learning love and acceptance for Chucky, his family learned love and acceptance for all people. While tracking the woods in Northern Michigan searching for the frost-bitten, lost-in-the-night little boy, they learned not to care that he teetered when he walked. They only hoped that he lived.

Chucky's family learned that life and love are not about intelligence or ability—that caring for someone who has disabilities teaches us about our own disabilities. It made them loving and lovable people. It made them stick together as a family, with a common cause. As it turns out, we are all PROUD to be related to Chucky!

This Thanksgiving we will all sit around the table. Chucky will tell over and over again about his job at the restaurant and about his girlfriend. He'll comment on football and politics and on some movie he's seen a thousand times. Chucky turned 40 this year. He still teeters when he walks. And once in a while he gets lost. But he has never seen the inside of an institution and he has experienced more of life than many 40 year olds. He has a loving family whom he has richly rewarded with his life. We give thanks for all the love we have learned from this special person. The key to the whole thing is that they had a "retarded" kid and stuck him in the middle of the family.

*This essay was written nearly 20 years ago, when the word "retarded" was not necessarily unacceptable or disrespectful. The decision to retain this word as written in the original essay was a difficult decision. Our hope is that the strong message of inclusion and respect is understood. (Janice Fialka)*

# *High School*

# A Self-Determined Athlete Achieves His Goals with Help from Parents, a Peer Mentor, and Open-Minded Coaches

Real inclusion of kids with disabilities occurs both outside the classroom as well as inside. This is a fairly basic principle; however, it is not always easy to make it happen. When our son Micah started high school, we thought long and hard about what after-school activities would engage him, keep him healthy, and help him stay connected to his peers in a natural way. As we explored our options, we were fortunate that Micah had a peer mentor, a junior in high school who helped us think through Micah's choices. J.J. was the captain of the high school cross country running team, so it may have been natural for him to suggest that Micah join the team.

"Great idea!" my husband and I thought. J.J. could support Micah in becoming part of the team. Micah would be physically active every day after school and would be hanging out with his new peers. Perfect! It never crossed OUR minds that Micah rarely walked briskly, let alone ran. But that was a minor point—for us. For Micah, running was the farthest

*Originally published in CEN Newsline, Vol 9, No. 4, June 2002. Reprinted with permission.*

thing from his mind. But he liked J.J., he liked hanging out with an upperclassman, and he was willing to try it "for two weeks, Mom."

Three weeks into the season (he made it beyond the two-week trial period—our plan was working!), we received a phone call from Micah's coach. He asked if my husband and I could meet with him to talk. "Of course," I responded, but my heart sank.

We set a date, but I knew what was happening. The coach was getting to know Micah and was realizing that our son was NOT a runner. My spirits dropped as I anticipated that I would have to "go back to the drawing board" to find something else Micah might do after school. Perhaps I would have to stage an "inclusion fight." It wouldn't be the first.

We went into the meeting prepared to be told that it just wasn't working out. The coach greeted us and then quickly began: "I want to talk with you about a goal I have for Micah."

"Goal," I said to myself. "G-O-A-L. Goal."

The coach continued. "I would like Micah to run one mile in one of the cross country meets in a few weeks. For those of you who are, like me, new to high school sports, cross country meets are five kilometers long, or about three miles.

"You mean you are not going to tell me it's not working out?

You mean Micah can stay on the team? You mean you have a goal for him?" I didn't say these things out loud, but I was shouting them silently. "Bravo!" I thought. We did not have to fight! We did not have to convince anyone that my son should be included. Instead, all we had to do was say, "Yes, Coach. That's a great idea!" All we had to do was let the coach work with Micah while we sat back in the stands watching our son run. We liked this a lot! To this day, I am sure Coach has no idea how thrilled and relieved we felt about his goal for our son.

At this same meeting, the coach made another request. He explained that during one practice a week, the kids ran for several miles in local neighborhoods. He worried that because Micah had a "bit slower" pace (those were his words!), Micah was often left behind and alone. Coach was concerned for Micah's safety. I suggested that on those days, Micah could skip practice and run with me at home. Coach quickly disagreed, saying, "No, I want him to remain connected with the school and team. I was wondering if it would be okay if he spent that practice in the weight room in the school gym, running on the treadmill." I was stunned to know that the coach truly wanted Micah's running routine to be as closely aligned to the team as possible.

Whaam! Another surprise—a welcome surprise! "Sounds perfect," I said, hardly believing what I heard.

I left the meeting pleased and excited. I met a man, a high school coach, who had probably never read anything by the

leading thinkers on inclusion, Marsha Forest or Jack Pearpoint, or subscribed to Inclusion News, but who understood "inclusion" from his heart and not from any mandate. He just "got it" and we were thrilled.

In mid-October of Micah's freshman year, on one of those glorious autumn days with a backdrop of blue skies, with orange and yellow leaves dancing lightly in the sweet, soft breeze, our son ran in his first meet. We videotaped all 11 minutes and 32 seconds of his run. Best friends came to watch, I choked back my tears of pride, and his team cheered, "Go, Micah! You can do it!"

In May as we began to think about Micah's sophomore year, we learned that his coach would not be coaching the next year. This news sent me into a downward spiral. When parents find adults who believe in their child, they cling to them like Velcro. I did NOT want Coach to leave.

At the end-of-the-year meeting to plan for Micah's sophomore year, we met the new coach. I eyed him suspiciously, wondering if he knew how terrific my son was, if he knew how desperately we wanted Micah to be part of this experience. I quickly learned the answer to that question. This new coach stated, in a clear, unwavering voice, "I have a goal for Micah. I want him to run in EVERY meet and I want him to increase his distance to two miles."

We beamed, nodding our heads, too stunned to find the words to express our excitement (again, no "inclusion fight"). Micah's reaction to the coach's goal was a bit different. He groaned, muttering, "Two miles! No way, Mom!"

While delighting in the day's success later that night, I thought of Adrienne Rich, a wonderful poet. She wrote about growing older and wiser and recalling the lessons she had learned along the way. She said, "I live now not as a leap, but as a succession of brief amazing moments, each one making possible the next."

The poem describes Micah's cross country story perfectly. There were many amazing moments, each building on the previous one. J.J., his peer mentor, opened the door to cross country. Micah's first coach opened the door to his first meet. Micah's second coach opened the door to running in EVERY meet and running longer. And this year, in his junior year, the new captain and a couple of other kids are driving Micah home from practice every day.

Everything is not perfect. "Real" inclusion is hard work, an ideal, something to move toward, something like a cross country run. Micah's cross country career evolved over time,

without huge leaps. Micah has learned that he must run every single part of the mile to get to his finish line.

There's a lesson in that for me, as well. All of us who believe in inclusion have to run every part of the inclusion course. I cannot leap onto the finish line without running the entire course (darn it!). Some of the tracks are smooth and straight; others have steep hills, twists, and turns. But each part must be run. Each part is connected to the previous section. Each part must be encountered, traveled, negotiated. As Micah has learned, we all must keep a steady pace, look ahead, keep breathing, be encouraged by the cheering, move forward at our own pace. We'll probably groan as Micah did: "Two miles! No way, Mom!" But we, like Micah, are spurred on toward our goal. There are no leaps in cross country running, but there can be many brief, amazing moments.

***The story continues***

A few years later, we ran into Micah's coach while shopping. We delighted in thanking him for his support of Micah in high school. He smiled when we told him that Micah still jogged regularly. Then he paused. A few tears welled in his eyes. He shared that he often thought of our family.

He explained that one of his own children developed a medical condition. During her IEP meetings, he remembered our advocacy and insistence of high expectations for Micah. Watching our family advocate then helped to pave the way for his family to be strong advocates for their child.

It was a moving moment that mattered for both our families.

# Nudging the Network

When our son Micah, who has cognitive difficulties, was a fifth grader, he was on the neighborhood basketball team. As parents, we were happy he was spending time with his peers, getting some exercise, and involved in a "typical kid" activity.

Micah participated in all of the practices and team activities and dressed for each game. The team and coach were supportive of his involvement; however, most of the time Micah only played for the last three minutes of each period. He was proud to be on the court, but it wasn't really enough time for him to get relaxed, engaged, and attuned to running fast while looking for the basketball. After the three minutes were up, the screeching buzzer would announce the end and Micah would return to his seat, having barely moved or touched the ball.

As the fifth grader season neared its end, everyone — from the coaches to the referees to his teammates— was planning to make Micah's last game the best for him. Their plan was simple. Micah would play most of the game. The teammates would constantly pass the ball to him. The referees would bend the rules…just a bit. Everyone imagined that at the final buzzer, the crowd would go wild and Micah would be carried off on the shoulders of his teammates.

The problem was that Micah hadn't really learned how to play basketball. During this final game, when the ball was passed to him, he reacted as if he were being attacked by a

*Originally published in CEN Leading Change, Vol. 6, Issue 2, 2007/2008. Reprinted with permission.*

flying saucer. He'd duck, slide to the side, or just be oblivious to the ball coming toward him. Without success, both teams became disenchanted with their plan and resumed their regular play, with Micah on the sidelines.

## Learning to Nudge

The experience taught us that we had to help the school and neighborhood include Micah in meaningful ways over time. It had to be an intentional inclusion. Including him in the game of basketball or the game of life couldn't be done all of a sudden and at the final stage—even if it was motivated by good intentions and love. We had to nudge! We had to sit down and have a conversation with the coach and the team to strategize ways for Micah to experience the game, learn the skills, and practice on a regular basis while IN the game.

Nudging, however, is easier said than done. We parents of children with disabilities often allow ourselves to get trapped by our discomfort and inexperience, which leads us into silence, anger, withdrawal, curtness, or aloneness—or sitting on the sidelines. As parents of children with disabilities, we must find the energy and courage to talk with coaches, our neighbors, our family, and our children. We must begin to form the words which will lead folks into conversations about how all children can play more than three minutes of each game. Micah and his teammates deserve to feel that kind of involvement and success.

## Applying the Lessons We Learned

Since that fifth grade basketball game, my husband and I have gotten better and more comfortable with encouraging community members, peers, teachers, and others to include Micah in meaningful ways. We have learned to hold conversations and meetings and to ask explicit questions, "What can we all do to ensure that Micah has a role in the action, an assignment, a part of the play, a ride to the dance, a meaningful way to be involved?"

## A Circle of Friends

Since third grade, we have supported a circle of friends with Micah. Although not always easy and clear, it has been one of the essential aspects to his successful growth and that of the entire community. The circle has changed in membership and focus over the years. The focus moved from making toys for sick kids in the hospital as a circle in fourth grade, to going to a Pistons basketball game as a circle in seventh grade, to planning how to dance with girls at the school dances in the 10th grade, to planning a school-wide program on disability issues in the twelfth grade. The opportunity to have a group of classmates was the right thing to do for Micah, for us, and for his community. It was this network that was the springboard to many successful inclusive experiences.

We've learned that it's okay—in fact, necessary—to nudge his network a bit. For example, one of Micah's personal goals for his senior year was to go to the prom. After little success hoping that he'd get a date or be invited to join one of the groups, we decided to nudge his network; that is, to make contact with his circle of friends. Soon we connected with one of the newest recruits to the circle, Shosh. As a fellow cross country team member, she wanted to include Micah in her group going to the prom. After many phone calls to the other 13–yes, 13–members of her group, Micah joined them, and thus achieved his most important dream of his senior year.

*Michael Boyd & Micah at Prom*

Getting Micah to the prom did not happen in a typical way, but it did come. We have learned over the years that sometimes you just have to bring people's wishes or dreams to the attention of others. There was intentionality behind this event, by way of many phone calls to the kids, to a few of their parents, and the intervention of a very helpful school social worker at the last minute. We've learned that this kind of careful but direct involvement, or what I've learned to call "nudging the network" is just the way it is and it isn't so bad. The kids were happy with Micah and he, all decked out in his tuxedo, had the time of his life. Like the other moms, I cried as we watched the long limo slowly move down the street, perhaps not with all the same thoughts as they had about their growing-up teenagers, but all of our tears flowed down our cheeks in the same way!

Although that infamous basketball game so many years ago might have seemed a game of defeat, it really was far from a total loss. We learned that many folks want to be helpful, but don't always know how. We learned that as parents we have to advocate for and with Micah to truly integrate him into as many activities as possible. We have to be specific in our problem solving. We learned that we can't be silent and hope for the best. We learned that it's okay to speak the truth to others and to ask them to think about some tough issues. We learned that we have to do it in a respectful manner that is tolerant of their unawareness of the issues. We learned that not all people will be on our side, but that you can find at least 13 teens who will say "yes" to having Micah in their limousine and will enjoy having him there—even if the evening took a bit of nudging.

*Micah on the Homecoming Court*

Since Micah attended the prom more than six years ago, we have learned a lot

about "nudging the network." Micah now advocates for himself on a regular basis and has his own group of friends from Oakland University. Many of Micah's friends have told us how much they learned from being with Micah at school, learning to be more comfortable with differences
in people. They learned it is worth the effort to get to know all kinds of people. Perhaps those are the real lessons of education.

*Micah and his friends at Prom.*

# A Word to Professionals about Parents, Transitions, Feelings, and Dreams

## A Teacher Reaches Out to Ease a Parent's Transition Worries

Several years ago, my friend's son, Andrew, who has Down syndrome, was approaching his sixth birthday—the first one celebrated in a regular education setting. Andrew was gleefully excited, as evidenced by his regular declarations that "soon, soon, I am bringing a big, big birthday cake with hundreds of baseball bats decorated on it to school for all my friends!" The teacher was preparing for the big day. She was also mindful that my friend was anticipating this day with delight, but perhaps with some sadness, too. The teacher found a quiet, private moment and offered these words to my friend: "I know how wonderful birthdays can be for families. I have also learned that some parents re-experience some less comfortable feelings, such as grief or sadness. Birthdays and other milestones sometimes call up uninvited feelings. I just wanted you to know that this might happen and that I would be here if you wanted to talk about them."

Stunned, my friend fought back tears. She wondered how this teacher knew what had been keeping her up nights. How did she know? The teacher had validated her private experience and helped her know that she was not a "terrible mother" for having those feelings of regret, loss, and sadness. Andrew's mom left the teacher's classroom feeling less alone and a bit more normal than when she had entered the school that day. She was not "cured" of her sadness, but she felt lighter, less troubled, more able to move forward. The teacher's insight and words of compassion were as beautiful a gift to my friend as were the 25 red and blue baseball bats my friend lovingly decorated on the cake for her son.

*Originallly published in CEN Newsline, Vol. 9, No,. 4, June 2002.*
*Reprinted with permission.*

## A Five-Minute Interaction Can Impact a Lifetime

This interaction took less than five minutes, but its positive impact continues for my friend even today, ten years later. Seemingly simple and sensitive interventions by professionals do not go un-noticed by families who often struggle to make awkward and conflicting feelings fit together.

Transitions, especially for young people with disabilities, seem to give rise to almost every feeling in the universe, sometimes all at the same time. Often there is no warning and very little public recognition of the universality of these strong feelings.

As my 17-year-old son, who has developmental disabilities, approaches his senior and final year in high school (gulp!), I find myself shoved back into that speeding roller coaster of feelings so dominant in our lives when he was a toddler and we were just beginning our ride into the world of disabilities. Ordinary moments now re-awaken strong feelings: a flyer announcing "College Info Night at the High School;" moms chatting about the rewards of having their teenage sons who drive cars run errands for them, seeing a group of young guys hanging out at the basketball court. Events like these can cause me to sink into sadness, reel into rage, and whirl into worry. Humbly I whisper, "I want those ordinary things for my son, too."

## Fight Back the Tears and Fears

Early childhood educators should have an awareness of and sensitivity to these strong feelings in parents. These professionals are well trained to understand the grief process during the initial diagnosis phase, when children are babies and toddlers and parents are unprepared for such unexpected news. As a result, early childhood professionals often address family emotions in skillful ways, giving parents opportunities to talk about their thoughts and concerns. Listening can help families to cope, adapt, and find their strengths. As the children move on into middle and high school, however, professionals may grow less cognizant of the normal, yet still troubling emotions that parents may re-experience during periods of transition with milestones occurring throughout the life cycle. It's not that these professionals are less sensitive, but perhaps they're less aware and more distracted by other educational issues and demands.

**Empathy from Professionals Can Empower Parents**

When school, vocational, and health professionals are empathetic and aware that grief is an expected emotion for most parents at any phase of our children's lives, we feel validated and empowered. It is helpful and tremendously supportive when professionals can reframe our parental feelings of evolving sadness and loss and recognize that, while these feelings come from a deep core of love and passion, they ultimately move us to create the best world possible for our children.

The next time you are working with a family, continue to create strong goals, clear objectives, fruitful action plans, reasonable time frames, and responsive interventions. They are important ingredients for successful transitions. But don't forget to take time to sit with parents, ask how they are doing, inquire about what might be on their minds, and invite them to share a bit about what they are wishing for or missing. Let them know that it is not uncommon for parents to feel moments of grief, sadness, loss, fear, anger, guilt, worry, and even despair. Allow parents the opportunity to sit with someone who can acknowledge the troubling emotions. Remind parents that grieving is a normal part of the parenting experience. Great comfort and strength come from being in the company of caring people who are not afraid of feelings. Feelings are at the core of our humanity—to bury them is to bury our potential to connect with others.

Marsha Forest, an educator and leader in the inclusion movement, observed: "Martin Luther King said, 'I have a dream.' He did not say, 'I have goals and objectives.'" Indeed, dreams are what propel us forward, and drive us to work harder. Of course, we need clearly articulated goals, but, ultimately, it is our dreams that breathe life into our actions. Parents appreciate it when they have the opportunity to work through their original dreams and move into the new ones. Rebuilding dreams is a lifelong journey, extending into every new phase and new milestone of our child's life.

If professionals move too quickly into action plans, they lose the opportunity to support parents through the phases of normal grieving, worrying, and wondering.

In Susan Zimmerman's book, *Grief Dances,* she poignantly tells the story of her daughter, Kat, who had Rett Syndrome, and the lessons learned by each member of the family in dealing with Kat. In one passage, Zimmerman's younger daughter, Helen, says, "Don't you get it, Mom? Kat keeps us from just living on the surface."

Professionals have that chance, too. When you pause, sit, reflect, inquire, and invite parents to share their uncomfortable feelings and worries, when you validate those experiences and value this part of your job as much as the well-defined action plan, then the work you do is not surface work. It is the stuff of which dreams—even new dreams—are made.

# *A Friendship between Two Young Men*

# Scott has a Good Mind and a Good Smile

*By Micah Fialka-Feldman*

Micah wrote this article about meeting his new friend Scott after attending the Toronto Summer Institute in 2001. It was published in "Inclusion News".

Hi! I am Micah. I am writing about a guy I met at the Toronto Summer Institute 2001. His name is Scott and he is 18 years old. He is a cool kid. He doesn't have eyes but he has three nice helpers. I like him. He is a new friend and a new pal. In Toronto, I went swimming with him. He lets us know when he wants to go swimming by moving his legs. I went to his PATH because I wanted to know more stories about Scott. It was interesting.

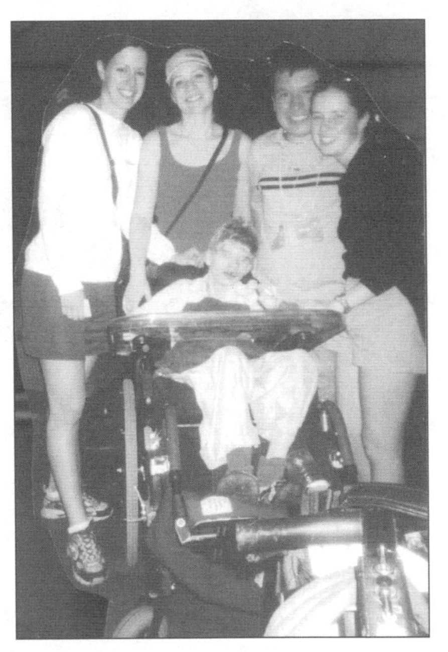

*Scott (seated) and Micah (third from left) and friends at Toronto Summer Institute 2001.*

It was fun meeting Scott at the Institute because he was close to my age. Different people have different abilities. Scott helped me understand that.

On the last day of the Institute, Scott's mom met my mom and they both cried like moms cry. They were happy. Scott's mom told my mom that the Institute felt like a bar mitzvah for Scott. I liked hearing that because I had a great bar mitzvah when I turned 13 years old.

About two weeks after I met Scott, my family and I went to Israel. I found a cool prayer shawl for Scott. Prayer shawls are important because Jews wear them when they pray. Marsha Forest liked wearing her father's prayer shawl.

When I came back to Michigan, my Great Aunt Joanne and Uncle Ross drove me to Canada to Scott's house. He lives about three hours from my home. It was fun to give Scott the prayer shawl that I bought in Israel. He was happy.

Scott and I went to the African Safari where the animals jumped on a car. We went out to dinner and I got to sleep over.

The next day I took the train home from Scott's house all the way to Windsor, ALL BY MYSELF. I felt happy that I could take the train. I had fun with my new pal, Scott. He taught me that friends can help you through good times and hard times. He taught me that it was easy to take the train by myself because he gave me strength. Scott is a nice friend and I'll be seeing him again. I hope I can see him at the Summer Institute in 2002.

*A month later, Jack, publisher of Inclusion Press, received the following update from Micah's Mom, Janice.*

Dear Jack,

Micah loves his story about Scott. Due to modern technology, his computer program is able to read him his story whenever he wants. He frequently takes advantage of this technology and often listens to the story several times a week. Recently Micah approached me with a concern about his story about Scott. He said, "Mom, I really think I wrote a good story but I don't like the part

*Micah (left), Scott (seated), and fellow adventurers*

where I said that he doesn't have eyes." He paused as he tried to find the words that would accurately communicate his worry. "I think that if some people read that part, that they won't really get to know Scott. They might not understand who he really is; maybe they would just see a kid with no eyes. I think that I want to change that part of my story and instead say, "Scott has a good mind and a good smile."

He asked me to make those changes in his story. I did, with tears in my eyes and respect in my heart. Micah once again demonstrated that his true intelligence could never be measured on any of the standard I.Q. tests. The questions used on those tests never inquire into the quiet brilliance of a young man who understands his responsibility to help the world see Scott as a remarkable young man.

Just wanted you to know how Scott's Story and Micah's Story continue in wonderful ways.

signed: Janice Fialka

*Micah planting peace pole for Marsha at 24 Thome.*

# My Second Story of Scott

*By Micah Fialka-Feldman*

Micah's second article about Scott was pubished in "Inclusion News" 2004.

In the last "Inclusion News" I wrote an article about my friend Scott. We met at the 2001 Summer Institute. He wasn't Jewish but his mom said that being at the Summer Institute was like Scott's bar mitzvah. A couple of weeks after the Summer Institute I went to Israel and bought a prayer shawl for Scott. I liked looking for one for him. When I got home I went to Canada to give it to him and then I took the train home ALL BY MYSELF. Scott gave me the courage to do that.

This is Part 2 to my story about Scott. Now that he had a prayer shawl, we thought he should have a real bar mitzvah because he was becoming a man (he was 19 years old) and he did good things for people. My mom, Scott's mom and I talked about how he would have a bar mitzvah. Scott is not Jewish but I am, so I could help. One day Scott had his bar mitzvah and it was a good one. Lots of people came and my dad got to be a rabbi for a day. He said that Scott is a teacher and professor because he taught people about love and friendship. Everyone told stories about how much Scott had changed their lives. We lit candles and people laughed and cried. And Scott's dad said, "It was all Micah's fault that Scott was having a bar mitzvah." I was happy.

One day I got a call from Scott's mom telling me that Scott was very sick. Then Judith Snow called and told my mom that Scott died. Later I called Judith because I felt sad. I wanted to see Scott one more time.

My mom and I drove for six hours in the pouring rain to see Scott. We got to his home at midnight. I gave Scott's parents a big hug. Then I walked quietly in his room. There were lots of flowers and candles. My friend Scott was laid on his bed. He looked the same to me but he couldn't go swimming anymore. He wore his suit and a dolphin tie because he liked to swim with dolphins in Florida. The prayer shawl I gave him was wrapped around him. I got in bed and sat close to him. I touched his forehead. He was cold. I wasn't scared. I was happy because I could see him one more time.

Then I went to sleep. We woke up early and put hundreds of flower petals in the casket with Scott. I took off all the petals off his hair and face because guys don't like flowers in their face. Then we went to church for his funeral. The priest put Scott's prayer shawl on his casket. He said that Scott taught us that all religions are about learning to love.

I felt proud to know Scott. He was my Canadian, older brother (I am one year younger). He was a good friend. He helped me get through hard times. I am still in contact with Scott's mom and dad, Gloria and Peter. I joke with them and tell them that I am their Jewish son. They came to my high school graduation party. I was happy.

After Scott died, Jack Pearpoint wrote me an email and told me to keep Scott's spirit alive and keep celebrating his life. I am doing that by writing this second part of my "Scott Stories." I will keep Scott's story around for a long time.

When Scott died, his mother said, "Follow the moon home, Scott." I like that quote. When I look at the moon, I think about my friend and brother, Scott. He was a good boy and gave us a vision of light.

# The Friendship between Scott and Micah A Mother's Perspective

When Micah was 17 years old, he and I attended our first four-day Toronto Summer Institute held annually. As Micah grew closer to adulthood, my husband and I wanted to learn everything we could about how to support Micah's ability to advocate for himself and live a fully inclusive and meaningful life. The Toronto Inclusion folks have been one of our family's most important guides. Micah was becoming a capable, proud, compassionate young man, all of which had much to do with what we had learned from Jack Pearpoint, Marsha Forest, Judith Snow and others at the Inclusion Press.

When we arrived at hotel for the Institute, we took the elevator to the 22nd floor. As the elevator opened, we were greeted with lots of sunlight beaming through the windows, colorful posters decorating each wall, and scores of folks greeting each other. The energy was buzzing. Micah immediately noticed three people who looked to be near his age and darted directly to them. He met Scott, who he described as "having a good smile and who used a wheelchair" and Scott's two personal assistants, fondly referred to by Micah as the "two really pretty girls." For the next few days, Micah participated in many of the conversations and activities, but mainly hung out with his three new buddies.

On the fourth and final day of the Institute, people gathered in the same large room where we had first arrived. The room felt even more colorful and more spirited with camaraderie and love. This was the well-known tender moment at the Institute when folks said good-bye and reflected on the impact of the four days together. When it was Micah's turn to share, he stood in the middle of the room and asked to have a song played from the CD he brought. He always seemed to select the perfect music to capture the meaning of the moment, and today was no exception. We listened to Charlie King, a magnificent folk musician, sing, "People like you help people like me go on . . . go on!" The message fit perfectly. No dry eye in the room, certainly not mine.

I wasn't the only mother crying. Sitting near me was Scott's mother, Gloria who had just arrived for the first time during the four-day Institute. This experience for Scott was a very important milestone for him and his parents, Gloria and Peter for it was the first time Scott had been away from them for more than a day.

Sitting near each other, tearing flowing, Gloria and I seem to becoming soul-sisters. Our mother-tears and our sons' friendship linked us almost immediately.

After the song was played, Micah sat back in the circle close to me, Scott, and Gloria, who turned to me and whispered, "I feel like my son became a man this week." Upon hearing her comment, Micah announced, "Then Scott should have a bar mitzvah like I did when I became a man when I was 13." Gloria nodded, smiled affectionately, and gently informed Micah that Scott was Catholic. Micah's elegant response was, "So?"

I offered a compromise saying that next month our family was going to Israel and we would bring back a prayer shawl for Scott, to honor his becoming a man at the Institute. Micah liked that idea and said he would pick one and "use it when Scott has his bar mitzvah." Little did we know then how much Micah would persist in his recommendation. At the conclusion of the Institute, we shared our goodbyes, promising that we would meet again.

Several months later, after returning from Israel with a carefully chosen colorful prayer shawl for Scott, we contacted Scott's parents about Micah's interest to visit Scott and deliver the prayer shawl. Scott lived about three hours from our home, which included crossing the U.S.- Canadian border. It just so happened that my aunt and uncle were travelling from our home in the Detroit area to Ontario, Canada near Scott's home. They offered to take Micah to Scott's for the weekend –

*Invitation to Scott's bar mitzvah, modeled after Micah's.*

*Mitzvah: doing good deeds*
*Tikkun Olam: to heal the world*

*Gloria and Peter Christianson*
*request the honour of your presence*
*at a celebration of Coming of Age*
*in a Bar Mitzvah Ceremony*
*for their son*
*Mr. Scott Christianson*
*on Saturday, the twenty-fifth day*
*of May, two thousand and two*
*at one o'clock in the afternoon*

to reunite the two friends and to deliver the prayer shawl.

Once Micah arrived, Gloria phoned us to let us know Micah had arrived safely and they were all "hanging out the hot tub together." I chuckled when I realized that I didn't even know Gloria's last name, but had a sense of incredible connection and safety. It was important for me and my husband that Micah was forming a friendship with a young man whose family passionately and skillfully advocated for their son to live a fully inclusive life.

Micah's return trip to our his home was a bit scary for me. He was taking a four-hour train by himself. Looking back now with all the traveling that Micah does on his own, it doesn't seem so remarkable, but when he was 17 years old, and barely able to walk cross the street on his own, it was an enormous step to take---maybe not as much for Micah but definitely a leap for his mother!

Over the several months, Micah and Scott, and our families visited and talked on the phone. On one visit, Micah brought the home video of his bar mitzvah celebration and service, as well as his printed invitation. Micah guided Gloria and Peter by saying, "You can use my invitation for Scott's bar mitzvah, you just have to change the names and the place."

Micah's persistence was unrelenting and eventually paid off. Peter and Gloria agreed to have a "Catholic bar mitzvah" for their son. Based on Micah's idea, they modeled the invitation after Micah's. Together our families planned a day of gathering family and friends, Jewish, Catholic and every other denomination, disabled, non-disabled, young and old – all to honor Scott's transition into adulthood. Micah was thrilled.

On May 25, 2002, about eleven months since Micah and Scott met at the Inclusion Institute, Scott's bar mitzvah was held. Over 125 people gathered under the outdoor tent at Gloria and Peter's home. Peter began by welcoming everyone and declaring with joy, "This is all Micah's fault!" Everyone laughed, especially Micah who seemed quite satisfied that Scott's bar

*Rabbi Rich and Micah*

## Where is it written you can't have a Catholic bar mitzvah?

*Friends and family gathered at the bar mitzvah. Micah, front row, smiling.*

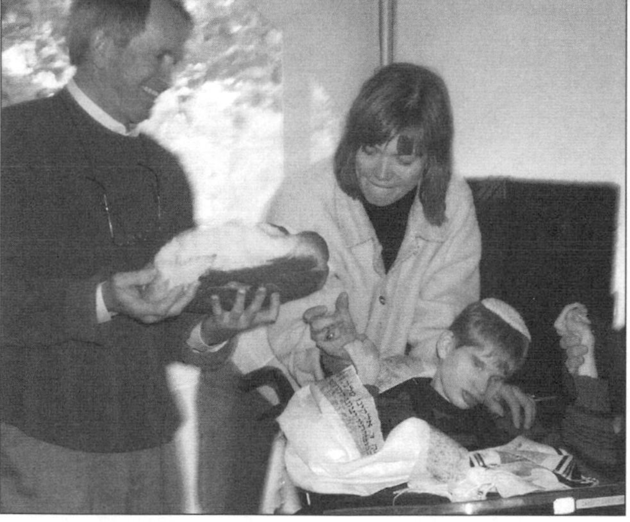
*Scott's dad, Peter Christianson; Scott's sister, Martha Christianson; and Scott in his prayer shawl*

## And now Scott is a man...

*Peter, Gloria and Scott (front)*
*Rich, Janice and Micah (back)*

mitzvah was happening! We planted a Peace Pole in the front lawn as we sang John Lennon's "Imagine."

Micah's dad, Rich, became "Rabbi for the day" and conducted the ceremony, which began with Micah proudly putting the prayer shawl around Scott's shoulders.

As in the Jewish tradition, a candle was lit for and by family and friends who are significant to Scott. Each told stories of how they knew Scott and what his impact was on their lives. We heard about Scott learning to swim, taking the school bus, riding on a roller coaster with his friends, and speaking in schools about his life with the support of his Circle. Despite the cold wind, no one left the tent for two full hours. Tears flowed, laughter bloomed, and candles burned. Rabbi Rich declared that Scott was not a teacher, but a full-fledged professor as evidenced by the deep lessons learned by family and friends. No one wanted the day to end – especially Micah and Scott.

In October, five months after the bar mitzvah, we received a call from Gloria that Scott was seriously ill and would likely pass in the next few days. Micah was very sad. At a workshop Micah was giving the next day, he dedicated his presentation to "my best friend Scott."

A few days later, our mutual friend, Judith Snow who had also been at the 2001 Summer Institute as a presenter called Micah and told him that Scott had died. Micah cried and informed us, "This is my first best friend to die and I want to be with him one more time."

"Of course, Micah." we said.

During our six hour car drive to Gloria and Peter's home, the rain never stopped. Per Gloria's suggestion, we drove directly to their home, as they had arranged for Scott's body to lay at rest in their home for 48 hours. When we arrived at 1:00 in the morning, we were greeted with strong hugs and a friend at the piano sweetly playing "Amazing Grace." Peter pointed to

Scott's room and Micah confidently walked into the candle-lit room. On seeing Scott's tiny body laying in his bed, with his prayer shawl wrapped around his shoulders, Micah immediately climbed into bed, laid next to Scott and tenderly place his arm around his friend, Scott.

Once again, Gloria and I sat next to each other, looking at our sons, tears flowing as that had at that first meeting at the Institute less than a year ago. Once again, our two sons were next to each other, bonded by the prayer shawl and memories of fun times together.

Reluctantly, Micah left Scott's bed after an hour to get some sleep before the funeral planned for the next day.

In the morning, Micah watched Gloria and Peter gently lifted their son into the casket. Gloria asked that we take petals from the countless flowers scattered throughout their home and place them with Scott in the casket. Micah made sure that none of the petals touched Scott's face. "Guys don't want flowers all over their face."

When we arrived at St. Joseph's Catholic Church, hundreds of people were streaming into the church. Many folks immediately noticed Micah and eagerly approached him with big hugs, thanking him for instigating Scott's "Catholic bar mitzvah."

Once the congregation settled into the pews, the casket was wheeled down the center isle. The priest welcomed everyone. In his hand he held the prayer shawl. He looked at the congregation and declared, "In this Catholic Church, this Jewish symbol of faith belongs here. I place this prayer shawl over the casket of Scott because all religions are rooted in love. Scott's life was one of love." Without looking, I knew that our son Micah was happy, knowing that his persistence over a bar mitzvah for Scott was always the right thing to do.

The funeral, not unlike Scott's bar mitzvah was graced with enormous love, tender tears, and a strong sense of a shared community.

Our family has learned so much from Scott and Micah. Most particularly, we learned that each person has gifts and when given the opportunity to realize those gifts, we all grow and benefit.

In some ways, the world would describe Scott as a "can't" kid. He could not speak, could not walk on his own, could not see, and had limited hearing.

However, those who knew him, loved him, learned with him, went to school with him, rode roller coasters with him, and hung out with him, would never describe Scott as a "can't" kid. There was so much he could do; so much he did do. Young and old found a calming spirit while in the presence of Scott. In fact, his high school friends often visited Scott when they needed what they described as a "Scott fix." They would lift Scott onto their laps, often share a bit of their lives, and sink closer into a peaceful state. Scott helped them to calm themselves.

Scott lived his life to the fullest, because he wanted to, he deserved to, and because his parents fiercely fought to have him genuinely included in his family, school, and community. Scott made long-lasting contributions to his family and community (as noted by many, including Rabbi Rich at Scott's bar mitzvah!) In so many ways, Scott lived what Ann and Rud Turnbull call "an enviable life."

Micah's relationship with Gloria and Peter continues to this day. Micah understood that he couldn't replace Scott. However, he lovingly offered to be their "Jewish son" for the rest of his life. They gladly embraced Micah's offer.

From this ordinary, and not-so-ordinary friendship, Micah learned about love, loss, and the fragility of life with Scott. Both of these young man taught me and so many others that there is power in taking risks, being friends, and pushing your parents to do the unusual.

"Really? A Catholic bar mitzvah!"

"Yes, "Really!"

And we are so grateful we agreed . . . finally!

**Post script:** In May 2015, thirteen years after Scott's passing, Judith Snow, our mentor and dear friend to both Scott's and Micah's families died. Upon learning of this sad news, and knowing that our family would be at Judith's Celebration of Life, Gloria sent Micah the following email:

*Dear Son:*

*I will be at the church at noon with Peter. We hope to sit with Janice and Richard and you if there is room in those pews!*

*Micah, yesterday at the crematorium Peter put in Judith's Casket with her body, Scott's bar mitzvah card. So she had with her the beautiful card with the photo of you and Janice and Richard and Peter and Gloria and Scotty. Do you remember what it said inside?*

***" NO matter who you are ,***
***no matter where you go,***
***we all need community."***

*We knew you would want to have been with us and remembered that you put the same card into Scotty's casket.*

*Micah, I had the most wonderful dream about Judith and I saw her choose to let go and move on her soul Journey.*

*It was beautiful.*

* * * *

*Moonlight on Clouds and Water*
*Judith Snow - 2007*

*"Late one night sitting alone on the deck during a Caribbean cruise I felt an eternal moment with the moon."*

Some of you will know of Judith Snow, and that among her many careers, she was an artist. This 2007 painting was featured in an exhibition: "Who's Drawing the Lines: The Journey of Judith Snow" in Toronto in January, 2016 - after her passing.

Micah and Scott, Janice and Gloria were all part of the Judith's world circle, and this painting seemed to speak to their shared connections through the moon.

# *IEP's Old and New*

# Thinking about IEP's

*By Jack Pearpoint*

We were talking about this book when Janice told us that she had just retrieved a box of dated Micah documents including many of his IEP's (individualized education plans). She said it was painful to read about his "IQ score of 40" and the relentless negative assessments that were part of the format of so many of these "required template" planning systems from schools. I jumped into the conversation virtually insisting that we include 'samples' of Micah's school records. Gentle Janice immediately leapt to the defense of teachers who were 'required' to follow these directives, and explained that there were some helpful contributions. I persisted saying that this was yet another Micah contribution. The IEP's had to be there to confirm that this remarkable son was really labeled, really did have difficulties, and often, his gifts and capacities were missed and constrained - not by bad teachers, but by systemic requirements that from the Inclusion Press framework are fundamentally flawed. Almost all system assessments begin with the assumption that people are broken and need to be "fixed". Then they "weigh and measure" all the flaws and brokenness, to assess what needs to be fixed most . . and then finally, if there is time, identify some small "fixing" strategies. Inclusion Press works from a foundation of giftedness, capacity and contribution. For Inclusion Press, a more powerful alternative is to develop a relationship with the same individual (and their family and friends), and by LISTENING for their gifts, build a "team" of capacity builders, who can individually and collectively discover and nurture a future of possibility for anyone - no exceptions. Micah's story is about listening and nurturing his inherent gifts.

By referring to a few of Micah's IEP's we are not attacking teachers who have little or no choice but to follow the rules. Our deep concern is that the assumptions under so many of these "tools" are actually harmful - not to mention costly in time and energy. This is a systems problem, not a personal criticism of teachers.

As we discussed this issue with Janice, she told us two short stories about Micah's sister Emma. When digging out the Micah records, they also watched several videos of Micah in his early years. Emma commented, "I never actually realized Micah was really disabled. He really was a handful. I just thought of him as my brother."

Today, Emma is a brilliant young teacher having "to do IEP's." It occurred to her that using Micah's actual records would be helpful in her teaching, not to replicate them, but to reveal the difference between the often well intentioned but "mechanical" implementation of planning, with her own remarkable IEP adaptation. Emma meets with families in their home, and through conversation and listening, creates an IEP one-pager report. Emma's summary simultaneously creates hope and possibility for an individual and a family, gives Emma a solid plan for her teaching support, and meets the system requirements. That is why we asked Emma to add another piece - based on her learnings from Micah - and Micah's IEP's.

So, Micah's IEP records are not here - because Emma's reflections about what she has learned - and how she has adapted her own teaching is what is really important.

# Reflections on the IEP Process and Special Education Meetings as a Teacher

*By Emma Fialka-Feldman*

## My Elementary Classroom

When I started teaching, I held my brother, Micah's story close to me. I knew who Micah was as a 30 something year old person. I knew about the current supports that surrounded his life in Syracuse, NY and I knew of the values that guided his story and determination. What I wasn't clear about, given that I was four years younger than him, was how he learned or what his behavior was like when he was an elementary student receiving special education services. He was my brother. I was his sister.

As an elementary teacher, I looked at the 6, 7, and 8 year olds in my combined first and second grade inclusive classroom. My students with disabilities seemed so far away from where Micah was in his current life. It was hard for me to imagine that my students would ever be able to live away from their families and communities or advocate for what they needed. The gap between where Micah was now as an adult and where my students were in my classroom felt enormous.

My students with disabilities were learning sight words, counting to twenty, and just beginning to figure out how to make connections with their peers. I felt overwhelmed constantly and discouraged by all that I thought they needed to learn in my classroom in 180 school days. I wanted to respect the individual journey each of my students was on AND I wanted them and their family to leave the school year holding onto the incredible options, opportunities, and possibilities for all people.

### Micah as a First Grader

During a recent school break, I visited my family in Michigan and watched home videos of Micah as a 7 and 8 year old. I was looking for similarities with my students and maybe even a few clues of how Micah was learning at that age. I read his elementary school IEPs my parents had signed. What I saw in the videos and IEP forms surprised me and shifted my thinking.

In the videos, I watched Micah, like many of my own students, move quickly throughout space. I watched Micah attend to conversations and show interests for very brief periods of time. I watched the exhaustion on my parents' faces as Micah sped from one part of the house to the other. I watched Micah be young. I watched Micah as a 7 year old. I humbly learned that Micah, just like me, grew up over time. I was sensing that I needed to have a more realistic understanding of progress and time for my students.

We all get to grow up and we are not who we are without the experiences beforehand. I read Micah's IEPs that described how he needed to "actively participate and organize meetings" (instead of sitting passively), to "ask and answer WH-questions," and "follow multi-step directions." There are still many things Micah cannot do, as well as skills Micah is still learning. Some of these skills are things that were written as goals in his IEPs over many years and other are skills written as goals in his IEPs that he now can demonstrate with confidence.

After viewing these videos and IEPs, my perspective about my students and my teaching changed. I realized I needed to be a more patient teacher, clearer on the skills I wanted my students to learn as 6, 7, and 8 year olds, and more confident about the values I wanted to share with my students' families ---values that I hope they would carry into their many years in the "Special Education" system. I began to feel more confident that we all, including my students, will grow and mature with time, support and opportunities.

## At the Special Education Meetings: Kevauna's IEP

With this new insight, I started attending IEP meetings with a renewed sense of possibility for how these meetings could be useful for everyone. I held on to my mother's words about the agony and frustration that she and my dad had at many meetings about Micah. I also held onto the voices of my special education instructors in my master's program who discussed how IEPs could be important tools both for the individual with a disability and for the educators who work with the student. IEPs are an unfortunate mix of too much jargon and report-reading and not enough of listening, goal setting and dreaming, and nightmare discussing.

At Kevauna's first IEP meeting in the spring, I remember feeling excited to share her growth. I also felt worried about how her family was making sense of Kevauna's strengths and areas of growth at school. Our communication throughout the school year had not always been easy. Kevauna was a student who challenged me constantly to be a better teacher. We sat in the "IEP room" surrounded by the speech therapist, the occupational therapist, the school counselor, the special education coordinator, the assistive technology specialist, the applied behavior analysis therapist, and Kevauna's mom, Tamika, and her aunt, Trisha. I knew Tamika was not familiar with all the people in the room and did not know they were all working with her daughter in some capacity. As was the standard practice, the special education coordinator started with some of the therapists sharing their reports. I immediately saw Kevauna's family sit back in their chairs, fold their arms, and maintain straight faces. I could feel the tension rise. This was not the new IEP experience I wanted my families to have. Data, numbers, and percentages flew out of the specialists' mouths. *50% of the time. Inconsistently. Not yet. Not age appropriate.* The reports with all the numbers did not seem to be helpful.

## A New Way to Share Information

I found a way to jump into the flow of the IEP meeting and

share my information. I know that IEPs can be overwhelming to everyone (eleven or more pages of information in jargon – how is that useful!!)

I was excited to try out a new way to share information with families at their IEP meetings. Over the course of a few months, during phone conversations with my mom, we developed a one-page sheet that contained some of the highlights of a student's learning as well as be a summary of what teachers and the specialists knew about the child. We wanted this tool to be meaningful, easy to read, and practical. Something everyone would appreciate. I refer to it as the IEP-one-pager. (See a sample following this essay.)

I used this new tool at Kevauna's meeting. Each person received a copy of her IEP-one-pager. It contained several photos of Kevauna smiling, drawing, and sitting at a table with her classmates. On this same sheet, I listed several things that Kevauna was able to do, what supports she needed, and our current focus.

When I shared this one-pager with the team, I noticed how Tamika unfolded her arms, and leaned forward. Her body seemed less tight. I pointed to the photo that showed one of the first times Kevauna wrote her name. A smile covered Tamika's face and she interjected about how she too was noticing more about what Kevauna could do at home. I talked about how far Kevauna could count to. I wanted Kevauna's family to know that she as growing academically. I have observed, too often, how special ed is about the student's social contributions. Kevauna should grow socially and academically.

Then I discussed the five short written sections of Kevauna's IEP-one-pager. I shared what she is doing independently, what she is beginning to do, and what she can do with support. I talked about what we planned to work on for the rest of the school year and I how these areas will help me write IEP goals that match her needs and strengths. Finally, I summarized the accommodations that have been most important. I want any adult who works with Kevauna to know that we must provide the right accommodations for her so she can grow her gifts and capacities. After I talked about the content on the one-pager IEP, the conversation shifted noticeably, and actually became less about reports and numbers, and more of a comfortable conversation among the team members. The specialists used the photos as examples of what they understood about Kevauna's abilities and needed supports. It felt that we were all getting closer to a more comfortable IEP meeting.

**Time Passes**

Kevauna is now 9 years old and after another year in an inclusive setting, her ability to sustain attention to tasks is growing. She is reading more sight words and beginning to add and subtract. She speaks more confidently and greater length. She is now a year and a half older from when I first met her. I do not know what she will be doing when she is 30 years old. I do know that she has twenty-one more years until then! And I feel more confident that what she is learning now will contribute greatly to her adult life.

When Micah was 9 years old, my parents (and me!) had no idea he would be a teaching assistant at a university, living hours away from home, and cooking with support in an apartment. There are many things Micah is still working on. Although there are no IEP meetings, his circles of support meetings and other planning meetings provide the opportunities for him to identify the skills he'd like to develop and the supports he continues to need. There is still a team of people who support Micah.

**Supports, Opportunities ... AND Time and Patience**

I continue to hold onto Micah's story as I teach, but now I also hold on to Kevauna's story. I hold onto the values that guided my family, and that influenced Micah's journey. And I hold on to the belief that time and patience are critically important. Kevauna is growing and we have yet to know all that she will become. My job is to hold open the doors of dreams and possibilities.

# IEP One-Pager: Kevauna's IEP plan - Emma Style

## Kevauna

**Things Kevauna Can Do Independently:**
- read (pointing to words, looking at pictures, return sweep) self-selected books
- raise her hand to ask for what she needs during whole class meetings
- identify letters, letter sounds, and numbers consistently and accurately
- follow a dramatic play sequence to engage with peers

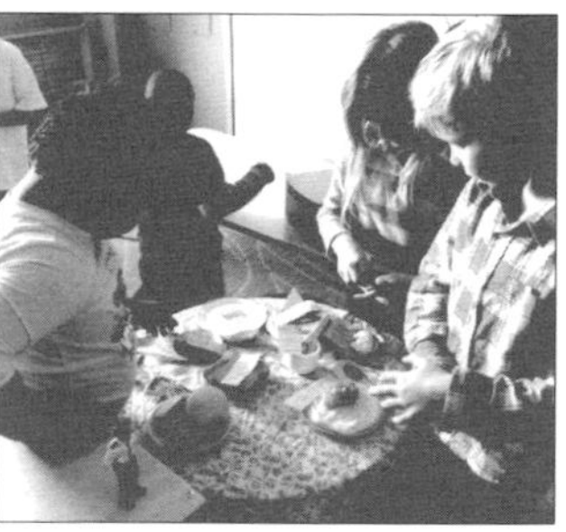

**3 Things Kevauna is Beginning to Do:**
- play math games with classmates
- write her name
- count objects showing 1:1 correspondence

**2 Things Kevauna Can Do With Support:**
- count beyond 15
- document her own learning on worksheets

**During the Spring, We Will Be Focusing On:**
- reading word families and increasing sight word recognition
- recognizing the total when counting
- using technology to support her growth as a writer

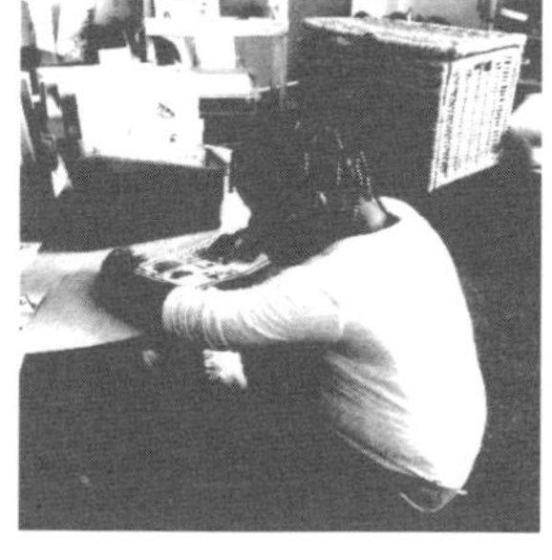

**Key Accommodations we use in the classroom:**
- multi-step tasks broken into visual & simplified steps, with adult or peer modeling
- use of manipulatives & multi-sensory approach to delivering content and instruction
- short, repetitive small group instruction with frequent breaks

# *College in Michigan*

# Detours, Not Dead Ends

## Micah's dream to live in a dorm

Following an hour-and-a-half bus ride, Micah arrived home late one evening after attending an evening college course at Oakland University, in Rochester, Michigan. He was exhausted from the long ride, but enthusiastic over his newest realization.

"If I was living in the dorm now, I wouldn't have to take two buses home. After my class, I'd just walk across the campus to my dorm. I'd be home right away and there would be other kids to hang out with." He beamed as he realized more advantages awaited him. "Then in the morning, I could sleep in, eat breakfast in the cafeteria and walk to class." He paused and confidently concluded, "I like that idea, Mom; that's what I want to do. I want to live in the dorm."

Thus began our next new adventure of opening more doors while politely changing the collegiate system. Micah, our 23-year-old son with cognitive impairments, is part of the new wave of adults with intellectual disabilities who are attending college courses and experiencing campus life as fully included students and citizens. His experience as a college student occurs at Oakland University in Rochester, Michigan with the support of the Options Program.

Being a college student over the past few years has expanded Micah's knowledge of what's possible and what options exist for him. During his first years as a commuting student, Micah felt little urge to live any place but home. He hardly knew what a dorm was and couldn't imagine not sleeping in his own bedroom. If asked, he would adamantly say, "One day I want to live with my friends, but not now!"

**Learning About Choices**

However, the more he hung out with his college friends, the more he learned about campus life. He watched them walk

*Originally published in TASH Connections, Vol. 34. No 3, May/June 2008. www.tash.org Reprinted with permission.*

back to the dorms and listened to their stories of limitless ice cream every night in the cafeteria with no parents looking over their shoulders. He began to understand that if he lived in a dorm he'd be surrounded by young people his age – and no parents.

During a tour of the dorm and while visiting friends, he saw the layout of the rooms, the location of the beds, the computers on the desks, and how to get to the cafeteria and lounge.

His emerging discoveries reminded me that giving people choices (Do you want to live at home or in the dorm?) is not enough. Micah had to be exposed to the possibilities before he could make authentic choices. He needed time and real life experiences to imagine a different life for himself. By being a college student, new opportunities naturally emerge over time.

But, as any family who has a child with a disability knows, making a choice does not automatically make dreams come true. You have to proceed with confidence and expect the unexpected. A lot of hard work has gone into making Micah's dream to live with his college friends in a dorm match the policies of the university. Unfortunately, his happy-ending story of living on campus has not materialized yet, but his dream is moving forward.

His first hopes took shape when he received an email from the University Housing Department informing him that his dorm application was accepted. His moving date was set for January 6, 2008. He immediately asked a friend for help to complete the paperwork. He "borrowed" the $100 deposit from us and then proudly delivered both items to the Housing Office. Later that night, he emailed his sister, Emma, using his voice-to-text technology. Emma already had one semester of dorm living under her belt. "I'm next, Emma," he wrote. "You have to buy me a new poster for my dorm room, like I bought you one."

We marked "Micah's Moving Date" on the calendar and prepared as best we could for this new and enormous change in our lives. His confidence and excitement grew with each packing box he collected.

## The Detours

That move-in date never arrived. An early morning email informed us of the university's new decision. Micah could not move into the dorm due to some overlooked university policy.

"I am going on a hunger strike on campus," Micah's dad responded immediately. We were all deeply disappointed. We knew how important it was for Micah to move into the dorm. He had worked towards this dream for more than three years. It was in his bones and he was ready.

It just so happened that Micah had scheduled his annual Person-Centered Planning (PCP) meeting for the next day. This meeting is designed to help him identify his goals and supports for the upcoming year. Micah arranged the meeting to include about 15 people, including several college friends, the Associate Dean of Education, some professionals on his PCP team, and the Director of the Student Activities Center where Micah volunteers. They met in a small room in the University Center with five large pizzas. Micah welcomed everyone and used his prepared notes to guide him.

Micah shared his accomplishments during the year, which included raising the most money for St. Jude Hospital and joining Alpha Phi Omega, the co-ed service fraternity. He then asked each person to offer a quick story of what they see as his achievements and his strengths. As Micah's world gradually expands beyond ours, it helps to hear how he is perceived and what roles he takes in his community. We heard about the contributions he is making in his student organizations, how his friends value his great sense of humor, and how he responsibly shows up at his volunteer job ready to work. Those vignettes are critical in helping us, as parents, "let go" a bit more each day. The observations from Micah's community let us know if he is finding his place and how others relate with him. We can see what natural supports are in place and what gaps we might need to address, both now and down the road.

We were grateful when the director of the Student Activities Center shared that Micah needed more challenges at his volunteer job. Here was someone who had great expectations for him and wanted to see him enhance his skills. As parents, we felt less alone in our pursuit of high standards for Micah. The team was able to creatively problem solve and identify a few other tasks that Micah could learn. One student volunteered to coach Micah with these tasks.

## You Gotta have Friends

As always, his friends—some of whom knew Micah for only a couple of months—proved to be the most important resources and problem solvers. Over the years, we have learned that any planning meeting should not be dominated in numbers or ideas by well meaning professionals who often are removed from Micah's everyday world and less likely to

make authentic connections or identify real-life solutions.

When we discussed the dorm issue, it was easy to see everyone's frustration. Rather than sink into doom and despair, several students (some hired by Micah as personal assistants and some buddies from campus) asked what they could do to convince the university that their decision was dead-wrong. One student decided to write a letter to the University President, asking him to immediately reverse the decision. The other students joined the chorus. Inspired, Micah said he would collect the letters and recruit other students to join in the writing campaign. The sparks of hope were igniting and unifying the group.

*Micah and his friends at Oakland University*

During the meeting, I asked Micah if he'd be interested in staying overnight once a week with a friend who lived in student housing. I didn't know whether Micah would want to do this or if a friend would come forward, but I felt compelled to find alternate ways to help Micah achieve his dream. I knew that one night a week wasn't the same as living in the dorm full-time, but it might be a small step—a stepping stone toward his dream. Micah said "absolutely yes" which was immediately followed by one of his fraternity friends offering the place. "Micah, you can stay with me. You've been at our apartment before so you know the scene. What's the best night?" As if remembering his first realization about the benefits of dorm living, Micah said, "Tuesday night I have a late class so I can just walk over to your apartment in student housing. Tuesday's the night!"

"No, you don't have to walk home, Micah," his friend offered. "It'll be dark. I can pick you up after your class."

Now I knew why this student's nickname was "Buddha."

In less than 30 minutes, several interim strategies were identified — all by Micah and his friends. Once again, I witnessed the "village" working.

## Lessons We are Learning as Micah Enters Adulthood

In some ways, they are many of the same lessons that we've been practicing and re-learning, and practicing and re-learning throughout the first two decades of Micah's life.

- **Our primary goal, especially as he moves into adulthood is to support and strengthen his *inter*dependence.** Let's face it. No one is truly independent, and in fact that is not what I desire for myself, my children, my neighborhood, or my world. Our success as a people depends on our ability to build community and connections.

- **To have dreams you must have real-life experiences.** Micah had to be a college student attending classes and navigating the campus before he could dream of dorm living.

- **Circles of support must invite, value, and engage peers.** The professionals and parents have to learn to "sit on their mouths" (Roman, 2003) and allow Micah's real community to find solutions and offer supports. This may require some expert facilitation and nudging to keep the conversation going, but it doesn't imply dominating the discussion.

- **A person's confidence is strengthened when their abilities are publicly recognized and expectations start high, and then reach higher.** When Micah heard that his friends were going to write letters to the university president, he was inspired to self-advocate and seek out other students to write letters. He is actively joining in the campaign for equal housing! And he was taking on leadership skills he hadn't tried before.

- **Never stop inviting and asking for help and ideas from a wide variety of perspectives.** I had no idea if anyone would come forth with an invitation to have Micah stay overnight on a weekly basis, but by taking the risk and asking, the door opened and stayed opened! Buddha came forth and now Micah stays every Tuesday with him. He loves his Tuesday nights with his college friends.
- **All supports can be instrumental in creating and nurturing authentic experiences and connections.** Micah had many of his college buddies at the Person Centered Planning meeting in part because one student he hired, an active student leader, introduced Micah to many people and organizations.
- **Relationships must be intentional and strategic.** Many people without disabilities have the ability to make connections wherever they go with very little effort. But for some people with disabilities, relationships must be fostered over time and may have to start with very intentional, almost artificial, mechanisms: Best Buddies, lunch groups, peer tutoring. But rich and authentic relationships can develop out of these intentional relationship-building strategies. Micah has experienced this over and over—as evidenced by his calendar!

*Oliver Hersey, a long time friend and Micah*

- **Parents can move from the role of caregiver to that of coach or mentor when others in the community provide practical support, encouragement, and resources.** Until others show up, parents can't sit down.

- **Our children really do learn by example.** Over the years, Micah has watched us regularly ask for help from others (though it wasn't easy to do!). We learned to reach out to others, invite them into Micah's circle, and provide them with concrete, practical suggestions to support Micah and his dreams. Micah seems to have watched and learned about self-advocacy from his family and from many other mentors. He now sends emails, makes phone calls, and invites others to hang out with him.
- **Serve food at all settings!** This needs no explanation.

*Alex Cherup and Micah met at Oakland University and now present together nationally on inclusion and disability pride. (Photo by Sarah Wentworth)*

## The Journey Continues

At this moment, there is no happily-ever-after ending of eating ice cream and living in the dorm. Micah, his family, and circle are working to change the recent decision not allowing Micah to live in the dorm. Meetings are planned and strategies are being devised. Through it all, Micah knows that he is not alone. He is a genuine part of a community who cares about him and supports him. Nor is it a one way deal. Micah too gets involved with his friends' dreams. Currently he is campaigning vigorously for one of his friends who is running for president of student government.

Micah has learned a lot from this experience—both disappointments and validation. He has learned what discrimination feels like, but he has also learned how to advocate and engage others to support his dream, and to never give up. His efforts took him on a path to Buddha, even if for only one night a week. Maybe that's true enlightenment!

Thank you to Beth Swedeen and Karen Hildebrandt for their wise assistance with this article.

## Reference

Roman, C.P. (2003). "It's not always easy to sit on your mouth." *Social Work with Groups, 25* (1/2), 61-64.

*Micah Fialka-Feldman on his first day of living in the dorm at Oakland University in Rochester, Michigan.*

## What's a Parent to Do? Micah's College Dream

My father proudly graduated from the University of Michigan in 1948, the first in his family of 11 children. Little did he know he established a generational pattern for the important men in my life. My two brothers, several cousins, and my husband all claim the same "maize-and-blue." At the age of 5, our son, Micah, attended his first U of M football game and was immediately awestruck by the "Go Blue!" spirit. I sensed he felt destined to follow in the footsteps of his Papa, father, and uncles. He didn't have the words to express this dream – words did not come easily to him then – but his dream was deepened with every U of M game he attended.

*Originally published in IMPACT, a publication of the Institute on Community Integration (UCEED) & Research and Training Center on Community Living, Autumn/Winter 2010-2011. Reprinted with permission.*

We as parents wanted both our children, Micah and Emma, to have dreams. Dreams motivate our spirit, drive us forward, stretch us in new directions, and compel us to try new things. We wanted our children to gradually feel the pull of passion and purpose. But what if their dreams are met with words like "unrealistic," "impossible, "out of reach," "can't do that," "unheard of," or simply "Why would he do THAT…..?"

Those were some of the very words we heard when Micah talked about his college dream. "Look at the facts," we were told, even by well-meaning people who cared about Micah. Fact #1: Micah has a cognitive impairment with a low I.Q. score. Fact #2: Micah didn't read or write (though he could sign his name after years of practice.) Fact #3: There were no fully inclusive college programs in our community. Fact #4: Youth like Micah, with an IEP, go to community-based programs after high school, not college! What's a parent to do?

**Listening to the Dream**

One of the first things we learned as Micah's parents was to listen to his dreams, even if they appeared "unusual." Our first experience with the "listen thing" occurred when Micah was in his first grade self-contained classroom. After four months he announced to us, "I want to go through the same door as all my friends." We were stunned, and later swayed by his insistence to move him into a general education classroom. Micah began to teach us "unusual" does not imply "impossible."

Getting Micah in a general education classrooms through 12th grade was a bit challenging. But "college" – that was something entirely different! We had no idea how we were going to help him get through that door. Nonetheless, Micah held steadfast. We were committed to listening to him and heard more than just, "I wanna go to college." We began to hear his unspoken desires like, "Hey, I wanna be with my friends. I wanna talk about what they're talking about. I wanna tell everyone what college I'm going to. I wanna go to football games. I wanna keep learning." And maybe most importantly, "I wanna make my own choices."

As parents, we shifted our thinking (most of the time!) away from someone else's facts and words like "impossible" and turned toward "what's the next step?" This was often not easy, but always right, and eventually became a strategy for dealing with the so-called impossible: Keep taking the next step!

**Building the Dream**

During Micah's final two years of high school, a creative and dedicated group of college and public school professionals and parents from the metro Detroit area met to consider, and eventually create, an inclusive program through which young adults with intellectual disabilities could become college students. Now called the OPTIONS Program at Oakland University in Rochester, Michigan, it gave students with intellectual disabilities the opportunity to attend classes, participate in extra-curricular activities, and, in Micah's case, live in the dorm. At age 19 Micah entered the program and through his six years in it grew academically, socially, morally, and politically in dramatic ways. He studied public speaking, created Power Point presentations on group dynamics, studied the difference between the ways males and females greeted each other in the Student Center for a sociology class, learned to use more hand gestures when speaking, studied social movements, took a hip-hop dance class, traveled to Israel, participated at the student leadership retreat, wrote papers (maybe not 20 pages long but two pages of facts he discovered with the support of a peer), and taught students how to use the voice-to-text software program critical to his communication. "Success" doesn't even begin to capture the extent of his growth, increased friendships and social networks, and enhanced skills to navigate the world. It wasn't a one-way street either. Based on the feedback from professors, staff, and students, he made important contributions to his campus and at several others across the nation.

*Micah with certificate of completion from the Options Program at Oakland University.*

In 2010, Micah received his certificate from the OPTIONS Program, celebrating his graduation. He now works in Detroit at the Michigan Roundtable for Diversity and Inclusion as a social justice educator for youth. He speaks nationally on disability and serves on the board of directors for TASH (www.tash.org) and the National Youth Leadership Network (www.nyln.org).

**Guiding Principles**

Looking back over the years, several principles guided our actions in supporting Micah's college dream:

- **Acknowledge the range of feelings.** For 12 years, Micah attended public schools. Although some days brought struggles to get him what he needed, the school experience was familiar and predictable. Near the end of his senior year, I had moments of sheer panic as I thought of Micah at college. Would he be safe? Would he be teased? Would he know how to get from one end of campus to another? He wasn't even comfortable crossing a small intersection by himself – how was he going to take two public buses for one-and-a-half hours to a campus? Feelings are part of all transitions. If we don't acknowledge them or share them with a trusted person, these emotions return, often hindering us from moving forward. It was very important for me to communicate with a couple of mothers whose children had disabilities and were older than Micah. They had lived through it, survived the transition, and knew what I was feeling and needed to hear. They understood and validated my fears, worries, and even occasional sadness. They also celebrated and shared my excitement. My mantra, when I remember it, is, "Feel the feelings first, with someone you trust, then move on to the next step."

- **Support great expectations.** This is a common chorus often repeated in the world of disabilities, so much so that sometimes it loses its significance and meaning. What these three words meant to us as Micah's parents was that we had to believe Micah could learn more and do more than what was often expected of him. Finding the right supports was vital to achieving those high expectations. "He can do more" became a common chant in our family, not in a way that pressured him (we hoped), but in a way that allowed him to build on what he enjoyed and could do well, sprinkled with a little bit of nudging out of his comfort zone at times.

*Amanda Rymiszekski, Micah, and Amanda Vanderford: Peer tutors and friends*

When Micah said he wanted to go to college, believe me, we never expected that he would eventually share a film about disability history in his class on social movements. We did not know that at the beginning of each new semester, he would stand up in class and ask for a tutor to help him study (and would be thrilled that "so many pretty girls" came to his assistance). We did not know that his confidence would soar so high that he would be able to speak on his own in front of the University Board of Trustees to present his case to live in the dorm. We did not know that he would sign-up to travel to Israel (gulp), or that he would discover a strong desire to read and diligently work at it with friends, or that he would find an interest in money, piqued by watching his friends use the on-campus bank. We did not know that he would understand the word "norm" and would inform us that it was not "the norm for college kids to wear boots in the winter!"

He became more capable almost by the day. Even brain research supports what many parents have known for years: Students with intellectual disabilities do not stop becoming smarter and better problem solvers once they leave their senior year of high school. They continue to increase their problem-solving skills and academic performance if given authentic opportunities to learn, embedded in high expectations.

- **Be mindful of the changing parental roles.** A wise sociologist once told me there are two roles parents assume: one is the protector and the other is the guide. In the early years of raising children, the parent defends, cares for, looks after, and shields the child from harm and danger. It is easy to see how this role is often more deeply entrenched for parents of children with disabilities. We

learn to be fierce advocates for our children. As they grow, we are challenged to move away from being the constant protector to being the emerging mentor or guide. We had to step back a bit and let Micah tell his story, hand in his un-perfect paper, sign his name at the doctor's office, make his choices about what to wear. This re-arranging of roles is not a simple transition. When Micah ended up stuck at his bus stop for two hours 30 miles from home in an evening snow storm that shut down the entire county, I wanted to put on my Super-Mom cape, leap over tall snow mountains, and fly him to safety. I couldn't. We literally became his guide (thank goodness for cell phones!) We created a plan whereby his father called him every 15 minutes as he stood in a bus shelter. (He did begin to think differently about the norm of not wearing boots after his feet almost froze that evening!) After that experience his confidence increased, as did ours in him.

*Micah and friends from Buffalo at the TASH conference.*

- **Build relationships with allies and his peers.** Beginning in sixth grade, Micah invited a few friends to help plan his IEP and attend part of every meeting. This involvement of friends continued into college. At his Person-Centered Planning meetings, he always invited a few college peers to participate by bringing real-world solutions and in-sights into the discussions. They often came up with the most practical and astute ideas of how to support him. When Micah was in college, each year we invited him and a few of his friends to dinner. We kept the conversations light and fun, and we listened a lot. We learned so much. Eventually some of the peers felt comfortable sharing more ideas and questions. I recall one friend asking me how to handle Micah's falling asleep in an early morning class. I asked her what she would do if another friend fell asleep. She quickly said, "I would elbow him and tell him to bring a cup of coffee to class." She instantly "got it" as evidenced in her response to me, "Oh yeah, I get it. I guess I can do that with Micah too." Folks need to know that it is okay to ask questions and share concerns. Micah learned to tell his tutors, "I'm okay with you asking about my disability. I'll tell you about it and how I learn best." Fundamental to Micah's sense of self was his participation in organizations led by youth with disabilities, where he experienced disability pride and culture.

- **Expect to live with uncertainty and risk.** I suspect that many parents raising a young adult with a disability have experienced a similar unsettling internal dialogue that goes something like this. "Do I let Micah try new things? If I do, what if something goes wrong? What if he gets hurt? Would I have this same fear if he didn't have an intellectual disability? But he does, so what do I do?" I'm not sure this worried-parent script will ever cease, but after more than two decades I am somewhat better at expecting these periods of anxiety. I try to be mindful of them, maybe talk with a friend or family member, create a plan, and eventually remember to not let fear dominate my decision-making and support of Micah. My husband and I try to minimize the risks, discuss pros and cons, and practice with Micah the best ways to handle awkward or uncertain situations. But, ultimately, we realize that overprotection will only hinder his ability to make safer decisions for himself. When this happened during Micah's years at college, I tried to practice getting more information from Micah, gaining a sense of how he was doing, and if necessary reach out to others. My husband and I cannot shelter Micah from all risks, nor can we do that for our daughter, Emma. Risk-taking comes with the territory for all of us.

I recently read an article by Sunny Taylor (2004), an artist with a physical disability, in which she said that too often professionals (and I would add parents) equate independence as having "self-care skills" such as feeding, dressing, moving about the community and banking. These skills can be important, but they are not the determining factor in one's quality of life. In her words, people with disabilities define independence beyond self-care skills as the "ability to be in control of and make decisions about one's life, rather than doing things alone or without help." Twenty years ago I don't think I would have understood this definition. I think I do now. Micah has taught us that the quality of his life is primarily based on his ability to know he has choices and can make choices with support. And for Micah, making his own choices has meant going to college (with or without his winter boots!) and it's been worth the effort and risk for all of us.

## Reference

Taylor. S. (2004). The right not to work: Power and disability. *Monthly Review, 55(10).*

*Retrieved from the Web site of the Institute on Community Integration, University of Minnesota (http://ici.umn.edu/products/impact/233). Citation: Weir, C., Fialka, J., Timmons, J., Nord, D., & Gaylord, V. (Eds.). (Autumn/Winter 2010/2011). Impact: Feature Issue on Postsecondary Education and Students with Intellectual, Developmental and Other Disabilities 23(3). [Minneapolis: University of Minnesota, Institute on Community Integration].*

# The Power of Inclusion: Personal Reflections on Creating Change

*By Shea Howell*

*What then would be our reason for instituting a program for students whose goal is not degree completion? The participation of students with cognitive disabilities on our campus indicates that we have a broader view of our institution as a center for learning... The liberal arts tradition maintains that higher education is more than preparation for a specific career or profession. It is about the continual quest for deeper understanding, richer life experiences, and personal growth; in short, the overused term – life-long learning. If we accept this as the role of higher education, then we must believe that this is our mission toward all individuals.*

*– Virinder Moudgil, Senior Vice President for Academic Affairs and Provost, Oakland University, delivered at Options Graduation Ceremony, April 19, 2010*

Micah Fialka-Feldman graduated from Oakland University in the spring of 2010, completing six years in a program designed to provide a fully inclusive university experience to young people with intellectual disabilities. With the support of Micah, his family, and visionary educational professionals, Oakland University opened its doors for full inclusion. In the course of this experience I was able to observe the power of inclusion to transform institutions and individuals.

I taught Micah in two classes during his final semester. He was in a public speaking class and I directed his capstone course. A year earlier Micah also took my class Persuasion and Social Movements. I was involved in his course selection throughout his academic career. I was able to watch Micah grow as an individual and to observe the impact he had on other students.

*Originally published in IMPACT, a publication of the Institute on Community Integration (UCEED) & Research and Training Center on Community Living, Autumn/Winter 2010-2011. Reprinted with permission.*

My first classroom experience with Micah was in Persuasion and Social Movements. This class fit his strengths. His family members are well-known activists and he has spent a lifetime surrounded by people engaged in movements for change. Micah has a keen interest in politics; he was among the most-informed students in the class and participated fully in discussions. During the class he was the first to have seen "Milk," a film about gay activist Harvey Milk of San Francisco. He encouraged classmates to see it and talked about how important it was for people to understand the struggles individuals faced. This kind of contribution was typical of Micah's participation, offering resources and insights to others.

Grades in that course depended on papers discussing some aspect of social movements. The only modification I made was to allow Micah to substitute video interviews for written papers. This did require giving him some clear direction in how to frame questions and approach issues. Generally, it was helpful for me to develop a few ideas and present them to Micah so that he could chose among them. He followed the same assignment schedule and handed in his interviews along with everyone else's papers. He worked with another student on their final presentation, analyzing his effort to overturn a university ruling preventing him from living in the dorm.

The second class, Public Speaking, also drew on Micah's strengths. During high school, he spoke to groups about people with disabilities. By the time he came to the university he had established a record of speaking events. Micah not only spoke on campus, but also traveled locally and nationally to make presentations to gatherings large and small. Depending primarily on Power Point presentations to provide structure,

Micah was comfortable as a speaker. In a class with mostly freshmen and sophomores he was among the most natural, organized, and effective speakers. Micah's main challenge was to move beyond material that he had presented and to explore new ideas. Here, too, the primary strategy I used was to develop some options for Micah so that he could select among ideas. While it was often difficult for him to generate new topic areas, once he grasped a direction he was able to move forward.

His final speech presentation in the course, on the use of the word "retarded," required research and organizational skills that challenged him. Working with his parents and another student, Micah crafted and delivered an excellent presentation, earning one of the highest grades in the class. More importantly, the speech touched off a discussion with students saying how much they appreciated Micah's perspective and how he made them think about things they had never considered. The experience of inviting people to think more deeply and to rethink old ideas are important gifts of inclusion to the campus community.

For the capstone course, Micah worked with Sarah Vore, a student doing a capstone in writing. Together, they produced a film about Micah's experiences at Oakland. Sarah and Micah met with Micah's family at their initiation and with Micah's permission. This proved to be an important support in developing the project. Micah's parents helped Sarah understand how to work with him to get his best ideas. They encouraged Sarah to not only help Micah frame questions for interviews, but also to be willing to challenge him. Having high expectations and not settling for less were important for their success in the project. Sarah wrote in her capstone paper about the experience:

> *Having never given much thought to higher education for this select group of individuals, my experiences with Micah have completely opened my eyes to the academic and social enrichment capabilities of those who are classified as*

*"intellectually disabled."(p. 3)*

Earlier Sarah described her first meeting with Micah and how she was able to confront her own stereotypes:

> *I felt both a sense of intrigue and enthusiasm as we easily made conversation. It was during that moment that my prior myths associated with intellectual disabilities were dispelled. (p. 1)*

Sarah's reaction to Micah was not unusual. By his senior year he was among the most recognized students on the campus. In chronicling the highlights of the graduating class, the Oakland Post, the student newspaper, listed ground-breaking for new buildings, a 9% tuition hike, a faculty strike, and "After covering his story for over a year, Micah Fialka-Feldman won his personal battle to live on campus..." ("Return the favor," 2010). This is perhaps my greatest lesson from this experience with Micah and efforts at inclusion. It is not only important for the growth of the individual, but also it radically challenges and changes the stereotypes of others.

Even in the earliest days of the program, the potential for altering thinking was clear. In a book chapter co-written by Marshall Kitchens, the director of the Writing Center, and one of his students, Sandra Dukhie, about tutoring Micah on the use of assistive technologies, they noted the benefit to Micah's increased confidence, but went on to say:

> *A primary benefit for Sandra was the sense of social awareness because of the project. Sandra describes working with Micah as "a wonderful experience." Over the weeks that they worked together, she says, she acquired a greater appreciation for individuals with disabilities: "I now have a better understanding of some of the frustrations encountered by many individuals with cognitive impairments." At the same time, Micah not only benefited from the experience in terms of communicative growth, but also from the social interaction, citing the social nature of the sessions as the most beneficial aspect. (p. 214)*

Micah's visible presence on campus resonated with other students with disabilities. In a moving article in the Oakland Post, Shawn Minnix (2010) wrote:

> *I thought I would take a minute to congratulate all of the seniors on their upcoming graduation. There is one person that I wish to acknowledge separately, and that would be Micah Fialka-Feldman, or as we just know him Micah. Micah has a cognitive disability, and is set to get his certificate at the end of this semester, finishing his odyssey and completing his education. I look at Micah and what he has accomplished and smile. He inspires us all to do greater things. I should know. In some ways, I used to BE Micah. I was placed in a school for the emotionally impaired when I was 6 years old, and I stayed there until I was 14 and it was hell from the start. I was told by my own principal that I would never finish high school.*

The full inclusion of Micah and other students required professors who were willing to think creatively about what would enable students to contribute and learn in classes. The single most important source of these strategies emerged from meetings with Micah, with his administrative support team of professionals, and with his family. Out of these meetings we were able to make adaptations that enriched the class experience for everyone. We recognized no one strategy fit all students or all classes, but through open communication and attention to the goal of full participation, we were able to find ways to meet the needs of all students. Adapting classes to meet the needs of students with cognitive disabilities took minimal effort. As a community we grew tremendously because of it.

## References

*Kitchens, M. & Dukhie, S. Chapter 9: Speech-to-text: Peer tutoring, technology, and students with cognitive impairments. In R. Day Babcock & S. Daniels (Eds.), Writing centers and disability (pp. 193-222). Unpublished manuscript.*

*Minnix, S. (2010, April 13). Underdogs succeed at Oakland. Oakland Post. Retrieved 12/8/10 from http://oaklandpostonline.com/2010/04/13/ perspectives/underdogs-succeed-at-oakland/*

*Moudgil, V. (2010). Unpublished remarks delivered upon the completion of the Options program, Oakland University, April 19, 2010.*

*Return the favor, rise up; If you stay or go, improve what was left for you: Staff editorial. (2010, April 14). Oakland Post. Retrieved 12/8/10 from http:// oaklandpostonline.com/2010/04/13/editorial/return-the-favor-rise-up-if-you-stay-or-go-improve-what-was-left-for-you/*

*Vore, S. (2010). Micah Fialka-Feldman. Unpublished senior capstone project (WRT 491 Internship), Oakland University, Rochester, Michigan.*

*Shea Howell is Professor of Communication at Oakland University, Rochester, Michigan. She may be reached at howell@oakland.edu.*

# Hidden Treasures behind Closed Doors

*By Janice Fialka and Richard Feldman*

When our son Micah was a toddler and being evaluated for his many developmental delays, a psychologist asked us, "Does Micah ever become frustrated when he can't do something or can't get something he wants?" Picturing our happy, mild-mannered child, my husband and I looked at each other and answered in unison, "Rarely." Micah was pretty low-key most of the time, content to sit and observe the world around him. He didn't seem interested in stacking blocks, or emptying drawers or pulling himself up on the furniture, activities that fascinated – and sometimes frustrated – his playgroup peers. "He's such a good boy," the other parents would say as they pulled their howling toddlers away from the allure of electric sockets or swinging doors, and we had to agree. Micah's contentedness was endearing and easy for us as harried new parents.

But later, as we reflected on the psychologist's question, a new idea began to stir in us. Perhaps a certain sense of frustration was essential to Micah's growth and development. We began to recognize that satisfaction would not spur Micah to try new things, to achieve more – to reach for the wooden block on the shelf or to coax his chubby fingers to grasp the ball. As long as Micah was content to sit, when would he walk? If we continued to anticipate his every need, when would he learn to talk? And so we began that lifelong awkward dance of parenthood, dancing between honoring who he was as a person and nudging him to try new things, to want more, to be dissatisfied with what he could do. Although it was often uncomfortable, we learned that we had to challenge Micah and encourage others to have great expectations for him too. We learned to embrace frustration as a precursor to progress.

*Originally published in the National Gateway to Self Determination Research to Practice in Self-Determination, Issue 6: Self-Determination and Postsecondary Education, June 2013. www.ngsd.org/news/impact-college-self-deermination. Reprinted with permission.*

As he grew and entered school, it was apparent that Micah liked to keep things easy-going. He didn't like being frustrated or seeing others upset and often tried to be the peacemaker. He liked being liked by people and won many friends with his contagious smile and concern for others. In third grade, Micah's insightful teacher told us about Howard Gardner's work on multiple intelligences and described Micah as being "people-smart," as evidenced by his attunement and responsiveness to his classmates. The teacher's description was empowering and reassuring to us. Children with labels such as cognitive impairment are rarely referred to as smart. But this wise teacher knew better.

Throughout his teenage years, we had a few flickerings that Micah had opinions and desires for "something more," but in the midst of sleepless nights we worried that he might not push to reach his full potential, especially if it might create hassles or dissonance for others. Micah's oft-repeated mantra was, "I'm fine. Everything's fine." Little did we know that tucked inside his sweet soul, hidden behind that magnetic smile, there was an emerging sense of righteousness and dignity that would ignite in due time, when it was really important to him. At age 23, he would demonstrate to us and to the larger world how profoundly motivated he could be when frustrated – in this case, by injustice.

## Opening the College Door

In 2003, when he was 19, Micah joined the first major wave of students with intellectual disabilities (ID) across the country who were attending college. He enrolled in the Options program at Oakland University, a fully inclusive program for students with ID. He got a student identification card, attended three classes most semesters, participated in student organizations, went on a student bus trip to Chicago to cheer on the basketball team at the NCAA Playoffs, attended the Presidential Inauguration in Washington, DC with his classmates, participated in the student leadership retreat and, in his own words, became "a college guy." After a few years of taking two buses each day to campus, and shortly after helping to move his sister into her dorm, Micah decided that he wanted the full college experience–including dorm living. In October 2007, he arranged for a tour of the dorm with a friend, and later with his dad and the director of housing. He learned about the cost of living in the dorm and the various meal choices available. He selected a meal plan that would provide three meals a day (including unlimited French fries!) at numerous sites on campus. He completed the housing application form with his father and with eager anticipation submitted it to the housing office.

At first, there was no frustration, just feelings of excitement as Micah anticipated no more buses, sleeping in late, and having 24-hour access to cable TV. Within a few weeks he received confirmation that his housing application was accepted and he was given an official move-in date of January 8, 2008. To secure his placement, he submitted the $100 deposit and marked his calendar with the big letter "D" which meant "moving into the dorm" (and "getting away from my parents, finally!").

But a few weeks later, my husband and I received an early morning email from a college administrator informing us that Micah could not move into the dorm due to "administrative issues." We sat at the computer stunned, reading and re-reading the four short sentences that would catapult Micah and the university into a two-year tangle of truth-testing and life-changing conversations. Up to this point, the university had been remarkably supportive, committed, and innovative in its full inclusion of Micah and other students with ID into campus life. The school was, in all respects, an exemplary leader in postsecondary education for students with ID.

In our efforts to understand this unexpected reversal of an agreement, we learned that an administrator opposed allowing Micah to move into the dorm because of groundless concerns that he might not be able to respond to a fire alarm, that other dorm students might be cruel to him, and that his move into the dorm might set a precedent that anyone taking even one class could live in the dorm. Each of these issues was unfounded.

In particular, Micah's ability to live in the dorm was predicated on his official enrollment as a student in a university-sponsored program. Later we learned that the university revised the housing form shortly after they admitted Micah into the dorm. The revision stipulated a new requirement that a student be matriculated in order to apply for dorm living.

Although Micah was an official university student via the Options program, he was not considered a matriculated student.

Micah was faced with a conflict. He loved his university, his classmates, his professors, and the administrators. Due to his friendly nature, he knew more of the campus community than most students. He also fiercely wanted to live in the dorm. How would he handle his intense desire – his right – to live in the dorm and still remain on a friendly basis with his college community? Micah had a history of opening doors, beginning in early elementary school when he declared that he wanted to go in the same door as his friends and be in general education classes. What would he do about this door – the dorm door – being shut in his face?

## Opening the Dorm Door

The following two years were a crash course in real-world advocacy and self-determination for Micah and his community. Micah had become frustrated and felt compelled to "do something."

He had grown up in the era of the Individuals with Disabilities Education Act (IDEA) and had been fully included throughout his school career. He also had been mentored by strong young activists with disabilities who had helped him understand disability not as a deficiency or misfortune but as a difference and a unique experience. All of these experiences came into play when Micah realized he was being discriminated against.

*Micah and his lawyer Chris Davis of Michigan Protection and Advocacy Service, Inc.*

Soon after hearing the unwelcome news, Micah, on his own, scheduled a meeting with a key administrator to explain his desire and right to live in the dorm. To prepare for this important meeting, Micah worked with a professor to talk through what he wanted to say to the administrator. He practiced delivering his major points with determination and respect. When the administrator did not reverse the decision, Micah met with other students for support and ideas.

With their help, he created a petition–and–letter–writing campaign resulting in 300 letters and 1,000 student signatures supporting Micah and protesting the discriminatory housing policy.

Next, Micah took a bold step and spoke at the public meeting of the University Board of Trustees. With dignity and poise he stood at the podium, thanking the university for opening its doors to him and other students with similar disabilities.

He explained that he was officially a student as evidenced by his enrollment in the Options program. He paid full tuition, participated in classes and student organizations, volunteered on campus, and had his housing application accepted and his enrollment check deposited by the university. He explained why he wanted to live in the dorm and why it was his right to do so. There was a hushed silence as he spoke, and our eyes brimmed, since there had been a time when had we questioned if he would ever be able to talk.

He returned to his seat and intently listened to the next testimony. It was given by a long-time member of the Michigan State Board of Education who joined Micah in praising the pioneering spirit of the university. She articulated the reasons why Micah had a right to live in the dorm and reminded the Board of Trustees and administration of the recently reauthorized Higher Education Opportunity Act (HEOA), which provides federal funding for model demonstration programs at institutions of higher education,

*Micah at friends at the Federal Courthouse in Detroit*

initiates groundbreaking policies supporting students with ID to attend college, and makes students with ID eligible for Pell Grants. She was followed by a passionate presentation by a disability law attorney.

Within a few days, Micah was informed via a letter that the dorm door remained shut to him and other students with ID. He was sad and mad (and frustrated) but undeterred. He met with friends and several student organizations to explain his situation.

With the involvement of many students, a forum was held to discuss the issues. The Sociology Club held a rally and marched through the student union holding signs and chanting, "Micah is a student." As news of the issue spread, formal and informal conversations continued, not only on campus but also across the country, discussing what it meant to be a college student. The university Student Council extended support, and Micah again addressed the Board of Trustees. This time many students – as well as faculty, alumni, and others – spoke on behalf of Micah's right to live in the dorm.

This particular university is not known for campus activism, but the issue of Micah's studenthood sparked the moral ire of many students, many of whom had attended public schools where full inclusion of individuals with disabilities was the norm. For those who had grown up living and learning alongside students with disabilities, having Micah and his Options classmates on campus and in the dorm made sense. For others, it just seemed right. Many students felt compelled to support Micah and speak out on the broader issue of discrimination and the

university's discriminatory actions.

After repeated efforts to negotiate with the university, Micah met with Michigan Protection and Advocacy Service, Inc. and decided to file a lawsuit against the university for discrimination against him. This was not an easy decision for Micah, and yet he possessed a clarity that took our breath away. As he emailed one friend, using his voice-to-text technology, "If I give up, most things won't change."

The next year-and-a-half included many meetings, a deposition, two hearings in federal court, and many conversations with family and friends. One of the most demanding experiences for Micah was the deposition, in which he was interrogated for five hours. The unexpected use of a video camera and the seating of the university administrator directly in front of him the entire time didn't deter Micah from answering the questions and staying engaged. Micah's lawyer said that Micah handled the undue pressure magnificently, answering each question with respect and poise.

On December 23, 2009, two long years after we received that early morning email blocking Micah's right to move into the dorm, U.S. District Court Judge Patrick Duggan ruled that the university must provide campus housing for Micah. As Micah put it, "The judge understood that I was a student." The victory for Micah and for the larger community was covered by newspapers and radio shows across the country, including NPR. He became CNN's Intriguing Person of the Day.

On January 4, 2010, Micah moved into the dorm. As we carried boxes of his belongings toward his long-desired new home, we were deeply touched by the many students and their parents who greeted Micah with handshakes and words of congratulations and welcome. Micah simply nodded, smiled his infectious smile and said to each person, "Thank you. I'm happy to live in the dorm." (To watch Micah move into the dorm, go to www.throughthesamedoor.com.)

**What Unexpected Treasures did Micah Find Behind the Door?**

Since December 2007, when we received the e-mail indicating that the dorm door was (temporarily) shut on Micah, we have heard Micah express the following thoughts. His words best reveal the unexpected treasures Micah gained through this experience.

- I got more confident.
- I learned I could do really hard things.
- I learned how to be a strong advocate.
- I learned I could speak out and tell my story in my words.
- I learned I could understand most of what my lawyer said, and when I didn't understand him, I learned I could ask him to repeat it in a different way.
- I learned that sometimes life is hard and doesn't make sense.
- I thought it was going to be easy. I didn't know it was going to take two years.
- I learned, "I can do it, but not alone."
- I learned what discrimination feels like and it isn't good. I learned I can fight it.
- I learned that a lot of people understood that I was a student, but not everyone understood that.
- I learned that I can talk to administrators by myself.
- I learned that people change their stories.
- I learned that professors can help me.
- My parents learned . . . a lot. They learned I can do hard things.
- I learned that when I feel upset I can talk with someone or listen to music.
- I learned why my parents and teachers taught me about Rosa Parks and Harriet Tubman.

- I learned that sometimes life is hard, and I am not always happy but I can get through it.
- I learned why it is important to talk with other people with disabilities.
- I learned that going through this fight helped me know that I wanted big things to happen for me and that gave me the confidence to move to New York and work at Syracuse University.

In the course of this two-year ordeal, Micah earned a Ph.D. in self-advocacy, so to speak. No PowerPoint or self-determination class could adequately teach what Micah learned. He lived it.

There was nothing glamorous about these lessons. Micah often came home troubled and confused about why he could not live in the dorm. It seemed so unfair; he was a student in every other sense of the word. He was forced to struggle with what might be called the existential questions of life: how to question authority, what it means to be a student, what it means to be human.

Living in this frustrating ambiguity, Micah learned the power of persistence, community, asking for help, and getting through tough times. He learned that when faced with adversity, it is important to connect, to converse, and to continue – not to hide. In reaching out to others, he heard stories about people who faced adversity and how they handled it. That inspired him to go on. Suddenly all the stories read to him at home and in school about Harriet Tubman, Martin Luther King, Jr., and Rosa Parks had real meaning to him and gave him direction. He began to see his story as part of a bigger story. He learned that sometimes there weren't clear answers, and that friendly people, people who smiled and said "hello" to you in the university hallways, could also discriminate against you.

He learned that smooth sailing didn't necessarily mean the absence of conflict. He learned that everyone has "life is hard" experiences, and that simply knowing that you're not alone can get you through the tough times.

As parents, we learned that we could not protect Micah from all the hard stuff. We had to "let go" (not give up!) and support him, often from afar. As much as we wanted to find that magic wand to keep him out of harm's way, we knew that he had the right to make his own choices, even if it meant "failing" or feeling troubled, sad, or mad. We can't say it was easy, but we began to deepen our trust that Micah could grow in his confidence and skills. We realized that if we tried to shield him from the frustrations of life, he'd never reach his full potential.

We are profoundly aware that Micah could never have pursued this fight without the support of others.

We witnessed the powerful impact this experience had on students and professors, both on campus and across the country, who rallied in support of Micah. We are indebted to Micah's attorney, Chris Davis of Michigan Protection and Advocacy Service, Inc., who always respected Micah and believed in his abilities. Chris never wavered in his professional obligation to "communicate with the client and to let the client set the direction at all times." He made sure Micah understood what was happening and what his choices were. He honored Micah's often-asked question, "But why?" and he appreciated Micah's need to have things explained in basic terms. Chris later told us how Micah's questions sometimes challenged him to think more clearly about what he said and how to articulate complicated matters in concise ways.

Two years is a long time to struggle with an issue. Honestly, we were uncertain if Micah would be steadfast in pursuing his desire to live in the dorm. We had assured him that he could change his mind and stop at any time; he had our full support and respect regardless of the path he chose. When he got discouraged, we reminded him that what he had done so far in pursuing his dream was more than most people ever do.

Throughout those two years, there was no guarantee that Micah would grow, thrive, and build his self-determination. But all those things happened when he faced up to his frustration and didn't back down. On the night before his federal court hearing, Micah sat somberly, still bewildered by the university's persistent fight to keep him from living in the dorm. He shook his head in disbelief at the thought that tomorrow he would be sitting in a courtroom. As Micah shared his thoughts and feelings, we sat perfectly still, longing to say something that would make it all better. We had no words, only the certainty that he needed us to listen to him. After a long minute of silence and, as if he was scanning the past 20-plus years of his

*Micah, Lawyer Chris Davis and family and friends outside the U.S. Federal Courthouse, Cinncinati.*

life, Micah said, "Since I was a little kid, I've had speech therapists, OTs, PTs, social workers, lots of teachers, counselors – all kinds of people in my life." He paused, grinned, and then continued, "I never thought I would have a lawyer too!" We burst out laughing as a family, the kind of laughter that heals, helps, and binds us together in hope and love. We agreed, "You are so right, Micah. We never knew that you'd have a lawyer or be headed to federal court."

Raising children with or without disabilities is a journey into the unknown. In our efforts to do our best to support Micah to be confident and self-determined, we stumbled head first into the great lessons of life. We – and Micah – learned that frustrations and closed doors are part of the journey and that they must be treated as detours, not dead ends.

*Living and Working in Syracuse*

# I Felt at Home

*By Micah Fialka-Feldman and Barbara Schloss*

Even when I lived in Michigan, I had heard about Syracuse University (SU). I knew they had a long and rich history of disability culture and that they trained their K through 12 teachers to work respectfully with ALL children. Then I got to go to Syracuse University myself to speak at two big conferences in August 2011 that were sponsored by the School of Education. I just loved being at a place that really "got" inclusion and disability. I really felt at home. I wanted to figure out a way that I could move to Syracuse.

So while I was still at SU that August, I approached Julie Causton-Theoharis, one of the conference organizers and a professor in the School of Education, to set up a meeting with her and George Theoharis (another professor). They told me to write a letter to Dean of Education Doug Biklen, indicating my interest in working here. That was the beginning of many long

*Originally published in the National Gateway to Self Determination Research to Practice in Self-Determination, Issue 6: Self-Determination and Postsecondary Education, June 2013. www.ngsd.org/news/impact-college-self-determination. Reprinted with permission.*

conversations about how both Syracuse University and I could benefit by my coming here. After the close of the two conferences, I returned to Michigan where I have been living for my entire life.

I was determined to make Syracuse my new home and I wanted it to happen by January. Many people wondered if I could make that dream happen in just six months. I couldn't think about IF I could make it happen; I could only think about HOW I could make that happen.

Over the next six months, we had several conference calls and Skype calls to discuss how we could work together. I knew I had to build my circle of support in Syracuse right away. At a conference I met Wendy Harbour who told me about possible job opportunities at Syracuse University. Then in November 2011, I visited Syracuse and spoke in an education class taught by Julie Causton-Theoharis. I introduced myself to students in her class and made more connections. It seemed definite that I'd be moving to Syracuse. I was excited.

**Planning to Move**

Once I had a job lined up and knew it was definite that I was moving to Syracuse, I posted a housing flyer on Facebook and sent it to my Syracuse email list--which was getting bigger every week! I found a place to live within walking distance of the university. I found someone whose roommate was moving out, and I contacted her. I was able to see the room and the house in November. Next, I had to find an agency to partner with. Jessica Bacon, Ph.D student at Syracuse, who is on the Onondaga Community Living (OCL) board, recommended OCL. I liked OCL because they believe in giving people choices and understand how to treat people with disabilities. They clearly believed in me as a person.

**Arrival Time**

I arrived in Syracuse on January 13, 2012 and have been working in the School of Education as a graduate assistant. I help teach a class in the School of Education with my friend

Michelle Damiani, a doctoral student. I also work with a program called Peer-to-Peer, which links college students with other college students with disabilities. I am also helping with a campaign called "I Am Norm" at Liverpool High School and am part of a disability rights group, Beyond Compliance Coordinating Committee, and a sign language club, both at SU.

**Taking Care of Myself**

So lots of things went great for me! I spoke up about wanting to move to Syracuse, and I made it happen, with help from family and friends. I got a job and a place to live. But sometimes I have to deal with things that are scary or unfamiliar, and I can get nervous about it. One thing that happened is when my housemate was moving back in with her parents, I had to get a new housemate. I heard that the new housemate was moving in in the middle of the night, and I did not even really know him! I was nervous and scared about that. So I called my parents, and we came up with some things I could do, like go spend the night at another friend's house the day he moved in. I felt better once I had a plan. He did move in - not in the middle of the night - and it went fine. But I was glad that I had talked to someone about how I felt.

Living and working on my own, away from the place I lived my whole life, means I have to speak up for myself and do what I think is right for me. I take classes at Syracuse University, as well as work there, and I had thought about taking a class in Disability Studies that sounded good. But then I found out there were over 100 students in the class! I knew that I did much better in smaller classes, so I chose a different one. I learned what works for me and that helps me make choices. Over the years, I have opened many doors with the help of many people. It all started when I told my parents that I wanted to go in the same door at school as my friends in second grade. Opening this newest door in Syracuse happened in just six months. Not only do I feel at home, but now I am at home, in my new home in Syracuse.

# My Brother's Journey: A Sibling's Perspective About College and What Comes Next

*By Emma Fialka-Feldman*

I love telling people that my parents, who reside in Michigan, live at least a day's car ride away from me (in Boston, MA) and my brother (in Syracuse, NY). This is a BIG deal. My brother and I visit each other in our different East Coast states without our parents. This is a BIG deal. My parents talk to my brother and me, at most, a few times a week. This is a BIG deal. Never could I have imagined that this would have happened. Instead, sometimes, having a brother with an intellectual disability, I grew up wondering things like: Who are Micah's real friends? Will he ever live on his own? How will he live a dignified life when most of society doesn't value him (and his label)?

In many ways, Micah had a picture-perfect inclusive K-12 education experience (this doesn't mean it was easy to create or actually perfect in execution). He had a circle of friends, he ran on the Cross Country team, he was elected to homecoming court, he played on the local soccer team, he won the social studies department award. Inclusion has always been a foundational belief and practice in our family. It was an essential part of Micah's education experience and unlike some special education students, his inclusive journey continues well beyond grade school.

However, it wasn't until he and I both went to college that something finally clicked for me as his sister. Inclusion became real and practical. Up until this point, inclusion made me feel good. In grade school, I felt safe knowing that Micah had things to do on the weekends, like his peers. It felt good

*Originally published in the National Gateway to Self Determination Research to Practice in Self-Determination, Issue 6: Self-Determination and Postsecondary Education, June 2013. www.ngsd.org/news/impact-college-self-determination. Reprinted with permission.*

knowing that Micah's peers cared about him. In the back of my mind, I had always wondered if people really wanted to be his friend (or did it just make them feel good)?

As we moved into college, inclusion felt more complex. I saw Micah being valued and I actually saw others grow in genuine ways as a result of having a relationship with him. I began to see people develop relationships with Micah because they saw the worth in who he was—not just because being his friend made them feel good. I saw Micah make decisions about who he wanted to be friends with. Suddenly everyone didn't have to be his friend; he and they could choose to become friends.

I saw Micah grow academically from the rigor of college. There were times when we were both taking similar courses and we'd talk about what we were both learning. He didn't "get" everything in the textbook (neither did I) – and that was okay. Not understanding everything is part of his disability. This does not mean that we lower our expectations; it means that we don't all have to understand everything.

College meant that Micah had to negotiate what his paid support-staff peers would do with him and unpack the tensions around "paying" a peer to support him. Inclusion in college meant that it wasn't always easy for him; the path was not paved for him – he had agency and self-determination in creating his future. He faced institutionalized discrimination; the college would not allow him to live in the dorms. He sued, eventually won, and spent his last semester living in the dorms. Micah's learning did not just happen in the courses he took. Like most college students, he also grew leaps and bounds from the social interactions and genuine experiences outside the classroom. For example, as a result of his legal battle, Micah now knows lots of legal jargon. Inclusion meant he grew as a result of his (real) life experiences, not the simulated life experiences in a classroom.

Like me, Micah got to test the waters of "independence" (or at the very least, had the opportunity to see if he could make

it without our parents) and develop the courage to continue to take risks. When he returned from a conference and told my parents that he wanted to move to Syracuse, this short statement seemed to reflect his entire history of being immersed in all aspects of life. As a result of his college journey, Micah had learned to create networks of support and advocate for his needs. Today, he wants to live away from our parents, create new communities, and be immersed in a community that he believes just "gets it" (disability, inclusion). He knew (and I knew) moving to a different state in an apartment with roommates without disabilities was not going to be easy. But he had the tools to make it successful.

I was excited when Micah moved to Syracuse in January 2012, but I was also worried. And as he continues on this exciting journey there are a few things I continue to worry about. Micah has lots to share with the world and especially educators. I hope that Syracuse finds a way for him to share his stories—what he has learned, not just about inclusive education but also about disability culture and disability pride. I think what makes his story unique is that inclusive education for him has been tied to learning more about his disability and becoming part of the disability justice movement. I know he can do more than be a go-to person at Syracuse--I think he can show his PowerPoint and teach segments of disability studies and education courses. This is going to take work on so many levels so I'm excited that he's surrounded by people who care about him and totally "get" him.

My worry is that his just being in Syracuse will be enough for Micah, that he will be so happy to be around people who respect him that he (and his community) will forget that genuine respect comes from being challenged to continue to grow. I am afraid that we will get complacent. That's my fear, my nightmare. I hope that he is able to find ways to connect, grow, and learn from the Syracuse community. That he is able to develop, to be challenged on his PowerPoint and speaking skills. That he is able to learn more about social justice issues. That he is surrounded by people who challenge him.Who tell him when he's talked too much about himself and when he hasn't asked enough questions about others. When his ego is gotten a bit too big (I say this with the most love in my heart). I hope people can continue to be real with him.

*Siblings Emma and Micah*

While supportive, nurturing communities that help people grow as people and as professionals are what many hope for, these communities are particularly important for people with disabilities. I think because the struggle to create inclusive communities is challenging, it is easier to be satisfied when we think we've finally done it (create the community); in reality, though, creating inclusive spaces and communities is always ongoing. Efforts to include Micah didn't stop once he was attending the neighborhood school, they didn't stop once he was playing on the local soccer team, and they didn't stop after he moved in the dorms at college. Micah continues to find more ways to make the world more inclusive for people with disabilities. It is process that forces him, our family, and our communities to grow and constantly strive to do better.

We're still figuring out this new chapter in his inclusive journey through life. I can tell Micah that it's not always perfect, that he shouldn't get complacent when it feels safe, and that he should continue to dream. And that he's got a community around him to help make the unimaginable imaginable and tangible for him.

# My Brother's Cap & Gown

*By Emma Fialka-Feldman*

*Micah walking across the stage with a big smile.*

On Thursday, May 7, 2015, Micah wore a cap and gown. He crossed a stage when his name was called, received a pin and certification for his work toward earning a noncredit certificate in Disability Studies, his name was listed in the Syracuse University College Graduation program, and his classmates, friends, trainer, college professors, and family cheered when he walked. In the official remarks opening this commencement, Dean of University College, Bea Gonzalez, confidently

*Micah returning to his seat with his friends and family.*

*Originally published in emmaff.blogspot.com. May 11, 2015. Reprinted with permission.*

and enthusiastically acknowledged the significance of Syracuse's InclusiveU program (the program Micah completed) and the students' participation in this commencement.

*Micah and Emma*

I have spent a lot of time this school year trying to unpack the social and academic elements of inclusion -- in a classroom where what I want, what I can do, and what may be "possible" conflict and meld together. It has been exhausting and rewarding. I have worked hard to figure out and think through what it takes to ensure that "all means all" -- from recess, friendships, counting, story problems, reading, telling stories, making mistakes, having consequences, and celebrating successes.

As I sat at Micah's graduation, I couldn't help but wonder about some of my own students. How do all families know what is possible for their child? How do peers know what their classmates are capable of? How do my individual students learn to dream, build determination, and constantly advocate for what they need to show what they are capable of?

After Micah's graduation, I went to a house party where dozens and dozens of people flooded the home. I knew maybe a handful of people. This was Micah's world. This was Micah's community -- his friends, his professors, his students he had when he co-taught courses in the School of Education. These were people he cooked with, people he went to bars with, people who he had mock dates with, people he stayed with when he was worried about his heart surgery last winter, people who felt loved, supported, and respected by Micah. No pity. No "buddy." No charity. Simply friends and community.

Micah reminds me over and over again that this work -- this work of creating the beloved community -- must involve intentional and authentic inclusion. Micah is who he is because inclusion (and Micah!) is working at its very best.

*Micah at his graduation party, looking at his phone.*

His inclusion has authentic age-appropriate experiences like wearing a cap and gown (he wasn't allow to wear when he attend Oakland University), like walking across the stage (some students with intellectual disabilities aren't allowed to walk across the stage for their high school graduations because they can't get the diploma until they age out of the system), like drinking alcohol to celebrate his accomplishment. These moments are not necessarily about an IEP goal or about growing academic or job-related skills. These are moments that allow Micah to see himself as a valued and respected member of his community. These are moments that allow his community to see his full participation.

His inclusion has intentional experiences like attending an inclusive university program that facilitates academic and social interactions on campus, like creating circles of support since he was in elementary school so that when Micah moved from Michigan to New York he knew what he needed to feel supported without his parents nearby, and like having parents that constantly, lovingly, and fiercely keep expectations and possibilities high so that phrases like "he's not capable of that" or "that's not within his IQ" don't limit him, like using technology so that he is learning what he wants to learn, about both possibilities and injustices in the world. These are moments that allow Micah to travel interdependently in his community. These are moments that allow Micah to see that learning is truly a lifelong process.

*Micah receives his Certificate in Disabilities Studies from Syracuse University and celebrates with family and friends on graduation day.*

# I Like my Life in Syracuse

*By Micah Fialka-Feldman with Nikki Conroy (2016)*

*"A community that excludes even one member is not a community at all" - Dan Wilkins*

*Syracuse friends Mike Fraser, Steve Singer, Micah, Brent Elder*

*Micah and Nikki Conroy became friends through Project ETHICS, a research project at Syracuse University in which Micah played an active role as an expert panel member, and for which Nikki worked as the Project Manager. In addition to their working relationship, they quickly forged a friendship. To keep Micah's family and Circle of Friends in the loop between meetings, Micah shares regular updates via electronic journal entries and utilizes Nikki to help make those happen. Micah finds this process to be therapeutic for sharing his thoughts and helpful for keeping his friends and family up to speed on what's happening in his life. In writing this article about life in Syracuse, Nikki questions and records Micah's answers. At the end of this article, they describe how they write together.*

***How long have you lived in Syracuse?***

It has been four years since I made the move to Syracuse, and I love my life here. It was a big move for me. I have learned a lot from many people that have helped me here. I wouldn't be where I am without help from my friends and my circle of friends. I am happy for the community we have made together. Here's a little bit more about living in Syracuse on my own, but never really alone.

***You moved to Syracuse because you loved how SU valued inclusion and understood disability. Do you still feel this way?***

What I like about it is that they train their teachers very well to work with people with disabilities. These teachers understand inclusion, and the students are in a place that they get challenged to learn and think about inclusion. Some school systems don't think outside the box, so it is good that the students are getting that experience here.

***When you moved to Syracuse, what were your goals? What were you hoping to accomplish?***

One of my goals was to be involved at Syracuse University and to help teach classes. And it was about being part of a community, meeting people and hanging out. If I didn't move, I wouldn't have had the opportunities I have had here. I have been able to serve on some projects and committees, and participate in group work.

And I have a group of friends here that help me talk about all the different things going on in my life. I talk to my parents, my sister, and my family, but I talk with my friends about things that we don't always share with our family. It's great that I have different friends who can help me with different things.

***What new skills have you gained or new experiences have you had in Syracuse?***

I've learned how to cook food. I've learned how to go skiing. I learned how to manage more responsibilities in life, like paying bills and rent. From living on my own, I've also learned more about shopping, like how to pick out new foods that I didn't eat in Michigan. I've learned how to ask for the help and support that I need.

I learned how to work with doctors to stay healthy. I used

to have a male doctor, and now I have a female primary doctor. And I've learned how to take medicine, and I have a great personal trainer too. And I learned how to handle getting big news; I learned that I had to have surgery when I was all by myself in Syracuse.

***That must have challenging. Tell me more about that experience.***

I was seeing a friend right after my appointment; we had already had plans to get together. When I found out, I knew I had a heart condition, but it was scary to learn that I was going to have open heart surgery at 29 years old. I had just met with this cardiologist for the first time, and he told me then that I needed surgery.

I called my parents, and they helped me talk to people for support. I spent some nights with friends to try to keep my mind off of the news. I had a great social worker who helped me to think about it less, to only think about it certain times of the day. Some of my friends threw me a good luck party before I left, to help me know that I was going to be okay.

I knew I was healthy and good, but I felt like my life might be coming to an end the day of the surgery. It was out of my hands, and I was wheeled into the room. It was the biggest surgery I've ever had in my life, but I knew that I had a good team. We found very good surgeons, and I was grateful for them.

***So you went back to Michigan for the surgery, and it went well. What was it like coming back to Syracuse?***

While I was in Michigan, friends sent me packages so I knew they were thinking of me. With people to help me, I wrote journals and I stayed busy. I had a social worker and a therapist that I talked to, and they gave me good strategies for thinking about happier things in life, and less about the surgery.

And I was diagnosed last fall with sleep apnea. I have a sleep machine now. I had to go to a place to get tested, and they told me that the test said I had sleep apnea. The sleep machine is interesting, but I do sleep better.

***And of course you had Circle of Friends before, during, and after the surgery.***

It's a great circle. Friends, people who work for me, and people from the university are part of my circle. I meet with them monthly, and I create an agenda for each meeting in order to check in about how things are going for me in Syracuse. At the meetings, we talk about how things are going with my job, and to see if I have any concerns and if there are new job opportunities for me. We have done fun social things together, like my graduation party and bowling, and we talk about dating. They help me meet other people. And I provide pizza for everyone.

***What have you learned about dating from your circle?***

They help me learn how to have nice dates, like going to a nice restaurant with a waiter instead of a fast food restaurant. I've also learned that I shouldn't have my phone out on a date because you're supposed to talk to your date.

***And you've had a housemate. How has that experience been?***

It is going well. I have had a lot of roommates since I've lived in Syracuse since I've moved four times. With my roommate now, it's great that we're friends and we can have fun together and joke. We have a fun time together.

It's interesting having roommates. With my other roommates, we had great times too. With one, we made chocolate chip cookies together. With another, I went to a comedy show. It's interesting how every roommate has been different.

***More recently, you've taken on a lot of exciting opportunities and experienced a lot of positive changes. Tell me about those. (It's okay to brag here.)***

I have always hired my own staff, but now I have more responsibilities with a self-directed plan. I sign their timesheets and determine what I need help with. I have a broker and a good team that helps me with my staff too. I have a fun time with my staff.

I'll soon be helping students learn about circle of friends and how they work, and I continue to teach classes at Syracuse University. I've also been serving on the President's Committee for People with Intellectual Disabilities. We meet in Washington, D.C. and will make a report with suggestions for improving the lives of people with intellectual disability. I also serve on the Board for TASH, where I teach people about working with people with disabilities, and I am on an advocacy committee for ARISE. ARISE is a non-residential Independent Living Center that supports people with disabilities in living independently. And I am Expert Panel Member for Project ETHICS, a research study about the ethical inclusion of adults with intellectual disability. I share my ideas about how to safely include people with disabilities in research.

***And you're a part of Dan Habib's latest film! Can you tell me a little bit about the film and how you got involved?***

It's about "intelligent lives," how people have to get tested, but those tests don't teach anything about the person. (What testing? Pretend I don't already know about the film and tell me about it.) Testing of their IQ, and how that doesn't teach anything about what someone can do, how smart they are, and how they can have high hopes and high dreams. But they may not know how to have high hopes and high dreams. This film shows them that they can think big and makes people see that people with intellectual disability can follow their dreams, like if they want to work at a university or want to go to college.

Dan asked me during lunch while we were at the President's Committee for People with Intellectual Disabilities, and he told me he was making a new movie and asked me to join. There are other movies, but he wants to show the real lives of people with intellectual disability, at home, at work, at school.

***What has that been like, being filmed?***

It has been fun and exciting, and cool to be in a film with a

*Nikki and Micah*

very famous and good film director. He made the great film, "Including Samuel". I think some of the good things are that he has filmed my whole day and my whole life in Syracuse, like my jobs and all the things I do here. It's fun, but it's interesting having a camera follow you around when you wake up, go back to bed, wake up, and being filmed walking to the bathroom . . . Dan asked me about whether I want to have children, sexuality, and some things that are usually personal. It shows that people with intellectual disability can talk about personal things, that they can want families, that they can be interested in dating.

But it's been really cool being able to share what I have done in Syracuse.

(Note: Dan Habib's new feature-length documentary, scheduled for release in the fall of 2017, challenges society's perception of intelligence. The film features Micah and other people with intellectual disabilities who are blazing a bold new path. www.iod.unh.edu/inclusivecommunities)

***What tips do you have for other people who want to move away from home and live independently?***

To be successful, you have to learn how to set up a circle of friends and how to ask for help. Sometimes people are shy about asking, but it's important to know how to get help from others. And make sure that you advocate yourself. Great things can happen as you advocate for yourself and get support from other people who care about you.

**How Micah and Nikki work and write together**

**Nikki:** I facilitate the process of writing as needed. Usually Micah knows exactly what he wants to write, in which case I provide the hands that dictate what he says aloud. And on days where Micah might be tired or have a lot on his mind, I sometimes prompt Micah with suggestions for what to write about, based on what I know is going in his life. In between journals Micah also sends me ideas for content via email so we

*Micah with retired Syracuse University Dean of Education Doug Biklen*

don't forget about them.

As for the actual writing, sometimes Micah and I talk out ideas before they're written down, particularly if Micah is still deciding whether something belongs in a journal entry or not. For example, sometimes there are things Micah is interested in sharing with others, but he hasn't officially decided whether he wants to send it to a big group in writing, or whether he would rather keep things to a smaller audience, like more private conversations with certain friends.

After some thoughts are written down, I'll sometimes give suggestions on how to slightly reword or reorganize the content so the readers can follow along more easily. Every suggested edit is run by Micah and approved before it's implemented in the entry. We cosign the entries, although I usually put by name in parentheses, "Micah (& Nikki)," and we send from his email address because it's his journal entry and people like to reply to him on occasion. For this particular piece, we had a brainstorming session where we came up with topics to cover so we could stay on track and have a more natural conversation. And then we reviewed together and made sure nothing was missing.

**Micah:** I journal because I want to share my feelings with my friends and my community. I feel happy that I can share my feelings with other people, and it helps people know how I am doing and what support I might need. Nikki and I pick the date and time to journal together, and then we figure out what we should write about. I think about what is going on that day and what has happened since the last journal. I like having somebody write with me, then I don't have to do it alone. It's fun having somebody that I can share my feelings with and what I have been doing that day or that week. We write the journal, and then we read it together before sending.

# The Syracuse Circle is Unbroken

*By contributing authors:*
*Jennifer Russo, Joanna O. Masingila, and Beth Myers*

## Micah's Circle of Support

Since Micah landed in Syracuse in 2012, his circle of support has probably been one of the best-facilitated and organized groups in the Syracuse University community. A cross-section of academics, friends, and professional support, this rotating cast of characters has met monthly to share Micah's experiences as he settled in his new community. The circle has listened and offered support as he progressed to graduation, worried through his health concerns, and now provides encouragement and the occasional nudge as Micah navigates job searches, relationships, and finding balance as a man in his thirties.

There's nothing particularly remarkable about the idea of person having a circle of friends, and those friends providing thoughtful and constructive dialogue. However, there is something special about Micah's circle of support, and that is the same thing that has helped him achieve personal success in Syracuse. The group shares a commitment to Micah, out of genuine love and respect, but also an underlying and permeating commitment to creating a fully inclusive society.

"It's nice to meet every month," said Sam Roux, part of the InclusiveU team at Syracuse University, "not just to hear from Micah, but also to meet with other like-minded individuals."

The faces around the table at Micah's circle meetings have

changed in the last four years, due to shifting schedules, friends graduating and moving on, staff changes, and Micah onboarding new "circle members" from his various professional and community roles. However, Micah keeps old and new circle members close and informed through email, sharing meeting notes, and journal entries.

"Micah runs his meetings with a timely and organized precision that eludes most professionals in my life," says Steve Singer, a doctoral student in the School of Education.

Katherine Vroman, a doctoral student, agrees with this assessment. "Micah runs the meetings, keeps to an agenda, delegates roles and responsibilities to attendees, and it feels like any other group of colleagues who work together towards common goals. Like other colleagues who are also friends, we work together on projects or research initiatives, divide and conquer tasks based on our unique competencies.

The longevity of the formal circle itself, and the fact that that the group has met consistently for years despite changing roles and circumstances is due to Micah's careful organization, for sure. But also, it has been lasting because the "support" provided is rooted in friendship, and that has extended far beyond the originally constructed circle.

Steve Singer says, "It has begun to feel like concentric circles of support to me, which feels like a good balance between natural and organized support."

For those who know and love Micah, and also believe in authentic inclusive experiences, it has been important to maintain that balance, even tip the scale more towards natural supports and social experiences.

"I didn't want to attend [circle meetings] as something to put on a resume, and didn't want my participation to change the reciprocal dynamics of our friendship," says Katherine Vroman. "Support goes both ways: I would give Micah a ride to trivia night and he would call to check with me to ensure I'd shaken my change-of-seasons cold."

There are so many metaphors that could be used to describe Micah's circle, and myriad of folks who are a part of it. One comparison could be to a wheel, where each person in Micah's circle has provided support, but also some sort if unique connection to the larger community.

"My role has been a combination of 'Other Jewish Mother' and 'Partner in Adventures,'" says Mara Sapon-Shevin, professor of inclusive education at Syracuse University. "Micah has been to my house to celebrate the Jewish holidays, and has been an active participant in cookie decorating, dreidl playing and ritual. We've also shared the experience of going to have Micah's ear pierced at the mall, picking out an earring and surviving the anxiety (his and mine!) that resulted in a gorgeous little diamond stud."

The Syracuse University community and culture is (and traditionally has been) progressive, inclusive, and accepting of all kinds of diversity. So, having conversations and interactions such as these – the ordinary goings on of daily life – but inclusive of a grown man with an intellectual disability, are not so unusual. It's just what we do at Syracuse. Outside of the Syracuse bubble, our society is still a long way from being fully inclusive, and individuals like Micah who are experiencing success will have many partners along the way who are intentional and mindful about the concept of inclusion. Not every person is so fortunate to have the family and friends that Micah does. But, his experiences and successes are illuminating what's possible in a best-case scenario.

Kellyanne Doherty is one of the professional staff members of Micah's circle. She has this to say, "I joined [Micah's] circle as a Medicaid Service Coordinator. Much of my caseload is for people's basic needs like a clean home, help with running errands and daily living skills. Sometimes this planning is really sad; I wish that there was more happening in people's lives. I worry that the vision for independence isn't possible.

"In [Micah's] circle I have the opportunity to think outside the traditional services. We are planning for a career and a life

*The Circle of Friends*

the way that any person would plan their life. I've grown as a service provider. The way each member of the circle works together and helps move the planning process reminds me that we can plan real involved lives for people. [Micah's] circle of support is what I want to see for all of my people, to reach their unique life goals."

I have stepped in and out of Micah's circle meetings over the last few years as an advocate, an employer, and also a friend. I think participating in the circle brings out the very best qualities in people, either by virtue of playing a supportive role, or just because one of Micah's talents is honing in on others' unique abilities. Contributing to Micah's discussions was always enjoyable, and I appreciate the opportunity to learn from Micah and the other very special people that have been drawn in to his circle of support.

## Micah's Work in the School of Education

*By Joanna O. Masingila, Ph.D.*

Intellectual diversity adds to the richness of our school and university. Having Micah as part of the School of Education and being a teaching assistant has allowed our students to not only learn about people with disabilities, but learn from and with people with disabilities. Micah's work with us is representative of the direction we as a school and as a university are moving – being inclusive of all learners and redefining what it is to be intelligent. Having a person with an intellectual disability as a teaching assistant in a higher education classroom demonstrates our commitment to diversity and inclusion, and helps our students learn that inclusion works when high expectations and meaningful opportunities are practiced. Micah is a valued member of the School of Education and truly bleeds orange!

## On Working with Micah

*By Beth Myers*

The first time Micah invited me to one of his circle meetings, I was not sure what to expect. I had participated in other circles of support before, but none were like Micah's. This meeting, held in a large conference room at Syracuse University, was filled with people who truly cared about participating in a process for their friend and colleague. Micah ran the meeting himself, ticked through his agenda, and asked for support in areas he needed. Each member of the circle offered something different, from dating advice to résumé editing. It was remarkable to see how skilled Micah was in gathering a group of friends and coordinating what he needed.

This year, Micah has been working with me as a Teaching Assistant for our class, Perspectives on Disabilities. While Micah performs many of the regular duties of a teaching assistant, such as taking attendance, preparing materials, and providing students feedback, I also consider him to be a co-teacher on many class topics. He is able to contribute a perspective that many people cannot. Micah's personal experience is invaluable to our students, most of whom are future educators.

When Micah teaches, the students really value what he has to say because he is able to personalize the disability perspectives they are learning in class. When the class learns about self-advocacy, they have a true-life example to explain the strengths and struggles of the disability rights movement. Often when a student has a question about a significant moment in disability history, Micah offers to contact the policy-maker, film director, or advocate directly because he knows them personally. Most importantly, Micah is very open to sharing his own experience with the students, offering them access to details about himself that many others might not be willing to share.

Micah also works with the Taishoff Center for Inclusive Higher Education, leading seminars for other students with intellectual disabilities. In these seminars, he shares his insights into self-advocacy and teaches others how to set up a strong circle of support. He offers encouragement to students who are navigating a complex social and political system around disability. Other students see Micah as an example of what can happen with high expectations and the right supports.

It is a pleasure and an honor to get to work with Micah. I have learned a great deal from him, and we are so lucky that our students get to learn from him as well.

*Jennifer Russo works in the School of Education, Syracuse University.*

*Joanna O. Masingila, Ph.D., is Dean, School of Education, Syracuse University.*

*Beth A. Myers, Ed.D, is Research Assistant Professor, School of Education, Syracuse University and Executive Director, The Taishoff Center for Inclusive Higher Education.*

# Teaching with Micah: Culture, Communication, and Ethics in Healthcare

*By Rebecca Garden*

I met Micah when he was a Teaching Assistant in an Introduction to Disability Studies course at Syracuse University, where I was invited to give a guest lecture. At the end of class he came up to say hello, and I told him that I knew about him from his and his father's posts on the activist listserv called Detroit City of Hope, and that I'm from Detroit, too. Some months later I ran into Micah at a community dinner, and he told me that he wanted to teach medical students. I said I'd think about it, but I didn't follow through. I think it was hard for me to imagine how Micah could teach students whose presence in medical school is hard-won through the sheer academic competitiveness: MCAT scores, GPAs, test score, the very measurements of intellectual performance that historically have excluded people like Micah from higher education. Despite my silence, Micah got in touch with me repeatedly and patiently, and, as I learned later, during the time that he waited for me to follow through with his suggestion, he went through his heart surgery and recovery. Micah was only temporarily sidelined by this however.

After he was back in good form, he contacted me again, and I set up a meeting with him and colleague, a pediatrician working with people with intellectual disability. She invited us both to participate in a grand rounds panel for the department of pediatrics. I prepared a short slide presentation and wondered about what Micah was planning. Uncertain about whether I was being intrusive, I checked in with him about the format, and he told me that I should ask him questions. On the day of the grand rounds, in a small auditorium packed with nurses, residents, physicians, social workers and others, I had my first encounter with Micah as an educator. Following my brief prompts, he described himself and his work as a TA and his experience as an activist, defined disability pride, explained how his circle meetings work, how he uses technology to comprehend written texts and communicate more fluidly, and how he was able to communicate with his healthcare team interdependently. My approach to prompting Micah's conversation was the same as I take to other interview or panel formats where I am moderator. I learn as much as I can about the person to be able to ask questions that will prompt them to reveal what I think the audience most needs to learn. Micah responded to each question and prompt, sometimes jumping in as soon as he got the gist, like when I mentioned assistive devices and technology and he replied, "Yeah, it's like, with like the technology now with iPhones and iPads, I can like uh talk into the iPhone and it will uh, print out on the screen and it has been like a great thing for me because the uh old technology I'd have to wait for somebody to help me do the thing or send like a message to my friends. But now like with the technology I can send them on my own and stuff." In response, I played the role of a kind of translator of the social model of disability for the audience, observing that Micah's use of technology "is a really good example of the social model where when we can provide support and accommodations it really expands people's capacities – it really supports their abilities. So it's a way of understanding how the social contours really shape what you can do." I think that the rapport between Micah and me or any person who interviews him is important to his performance in a setting like this grand rounds. I am conscious of the ways in which my questions and prompts and my "translations," my glosses on what Micah has said, can dominate or manage his self-expression rather than just facilitate it. This is true in any interview or panel format but particularly true when there is an implicit power balance at play in the dialogue. In this case, my PhD and status as a professor in the medical school where the grand rounds took place ascribed me greater power. At a disability studies/rights conference, I think Micah would have more social capital and authority than I. Nonetheless, Micah held his own in a setting where the medical model of disability dominates and critiques of power are almost entirely absent.

*Micah's team—Christy Kalebic, Carly Maldonado, and Jody Taylor*

Micah was confident and calm and held his own amongst clinicians who value confidence and nerve as much as intellectual achievement and test scores. And, like most clinicians, Micah is ambitious. So he got in touch with me again to have lunch and talk about other ways that he might teach medical students. I ended up designing a new course (for nursing rather than medical students) where Micah and two other people who play critical roles in the Syracuse community would work with my students as Community Educators.

**"Culture Communication & Ethics in Healthcare: Deaf & Disability Studies Approaches"** is a course that took place in the Fall of 2015 and included nursing students from SUNY Upstate Medical University and students from Syracuse University from collaborative industrial design, public health, psychology, disability studies, education, and audiology. A core participant and co-leader of discussions was Prof. Michael Schwartz of Syracuse University's College of Law. Michael is deaf and got his PhD in disability studies doing important research on the experiences of deaf people in healthcare. The other Community Educators were Mable Wilson, a community gardener and community activist in Syracuse who helped to found an organization that supports over 20 community gardens in the city, and Monu Chhetri, a deaf-Nepalese New American who provides communication access for roughly 50 deaf Nepalese immigrants and has organized a weekly community meeting for a wide range of deaf New Americans.

I immersed my students in deaf studies and critical disability studies, research on disparities involving deaf and disabled patients in healthcare, and interviewing techniques. After five weeks of preparation, I brought the Community Educators onto campus, where the students were grouped into small teams and worked together in a classroom with one Educator. Micah's team—Christy Kalebic, Carly Maldonado, and Jody Taylor—asked him questions using an interview guide the entire class developed together. They asked about how he describes his community and how he understands his own identity (and he had more than one: as an educator, a disability rights activist, as a Jew and a member of the Hillel community on campus), experiences of access and barriers, and experiences of healthcare.

Through the interview, Micah's team learned about his identities as an educator, educating people about disability and disability pride, his role as an advocate, providing support and advice for other disabled people and working with them to make change, and his approach to access, especially how technology and the circle of support shape his experience of community and his independence. One student observed that Micah's identity is not shaped by *"historical measurements of disabled people,"* but rather through his *"his engagements, abilities, and capabilities" (Taylor).* Another student drew on disability studies theory to demonstrate how technology extends all human capacities, which helped her to better appreciate Micah's statement that *"I have a disability, but I have great technology that helps me."* The student observes that, *"Just as*

*Micah's iPhone 'extends human capacities' and enables him to make his way in the world more easily, our iPhones do the same thing" (Maldonado).*

Micah taught the students about how he works interdependently with his staff and others when accessing healthcare:

> *His staff is a very important support system and provide communication support for Micah. For significant appointments...he prefers his staff to come into the room to listen and take notes. For simple physicals or exams, he requests that his staff remain in the waiting room.... Slow down and make sure the patient knows exactly what is going on. Sometimes, people with intellectual or cognitive disabilities especially, but not only, may need to go home to consult others and work out a decision instead of making one right there. Also, to make sure patients understand exactly how any procedure they're having is going to occur. This is true of anyone; everyone wants a comprehensive understanding of anything that is going to happen to them, particularly medically. Big decisions shouldn't be made on the spot, either, and especially without consult. Patients can be in shock when they receive serious information, and their decision-making will be clouded, so it is important to ensure people make well-informed decisions. In order to thoroughly communicate information about procedures, Micah suggested visual aids, such as diagrams, in addition to a step-by-step run through. (Kalebic)*

Most critically, students realized that insights from Micah are applicable to all people who seek healthcare. Describing how Micah moved forward after a physician gave him a serious and frightening diagnosis when he had gone alone to an appointment for what he thought was simply a checkup, one student wrote:

> *His current approach to the medical system, considering his previous experience, is a perfect example of how negative experiences can shift communication dynamics: 'When I go to the doctor's office I tend to make notes or have my staff take notes...It's always good to send it to my parents or do research'*

> *(Fialka-Feldman, 2015). He uses this as a way to make use that he understands exactly what is said and to make sure he records what the doctors says about his health. A common problem many of us face is that when we walk out of the doctor's office we tend to forget what he or she said, the instructions given, or just generally regret not making notes and asking follow up questions when you do remember. We tend to be so focused on quickly processing what the doctor said in that short period of time that we tend to not ask questions. However, it is how you choose to change the dynamics and shift the consciousness that makes a difference in the future. The shift can be having access to support whether physical (personal) or technological support to assist in this regard. (Taylor)*

Micah's role as a Community Educator in my "Culture, Communication, and Healthcare" course was one that worked as a powerful influence on students, suggesting to them how we can "change the dynamics and shift the consciousness" to make a difference, right now and in the future. This happened because of Micah's skill at educating me. He worked patiently, interacting with me over a series of encounters until I could shift my imagination beyond my initial limited framing of the question of Micah teaching in healthcare education to a design of a course. Community Educators like Micah help educators and students to explore not only difference and disparities but also how a range of identities and embodiments can open up our schooling, our work, and the processes by which we build communities and support those within it.

*Rebecca Garden, Ph.D is Associate Professor of Bioethics & Humanities*
*SUNY Upstate Medical University*

# *Family Interviews*

## Interviewing Janice, Micah and Emma

*by Mark Larson*

A few years ago, I was trying to get hold of the late, philosopher and activist, Grace Lee Boggs in Detroit. I wanted to add her to my collection of interviews on education that would appear on my website, American Stories Continuum (http://americanstoriescontinuum.com/). I was directed to Richard Feldman who had worked closely with her. When I talked with Rich on the phone, he said he'd set this up for me and then said, "You really should talk to my wife, Janice. She's got an important story, too." And that was my first glimpse of how the Feldman-Fialka family works. As a team of tireless advocates for one another and for the fundamental matter of inclusion.

Janice's interview, included here, is derived from a long phone conversation I had with her in 2012. I remember sitting on my back deck and being taken aback by her candor and her poignant, unpretentious generosity of spirit. After talking with Janice, I wanted to speak to both of her adult children, Emma and Micah. My original idea was to use their interviews within Janice's, but both Emma's and Micah's stories were just as thoughtful and available as Janice's. Clearly, all three conversations would stand on their own, which is why there are three separate but adjacent interviews here. I believe the three, read together, form a single and powerful message about what inclusion really means and why it matters.

My conversations and subsequent in-person meetings with the Fialka-Feldman family (I now consider them dear friends) have transformed my notions of inclusion and community. I talked with Emma once about my struggle to capture Micah's tendency, at the time, to say "you know" a lot and to repeat phrases over and over before he got to his point. I wanted to capture his unique rhythms, his authentic voice without

*Originally published in American Stories Continuum, 2016.*
*www.americanstoriescontinuum.com Reprinted with permission.*

making it seem like I was inadvertently mocking him. Emma forever opened my world when she said she appreciated that I was trying to capture who Micah really is. At that moment, I understood that inclusion is only true inclusion if it embraces every aspect of a person rather who we feel they should be.

At the end of my conversation with Janice, she paid me the finest compliment I have ever received in this work: "Can I just tell you," she said, "you make it hard for me not to tell you things." But it wasn't me; it was Janice's broad embrace and the ways she and her family seem to interact with the world. It was not that I made it hard for Janice not to tell me things. It's that she made it easy for me listen and to hear. That, I think, is the lasting gift of Janice Fialka and her family to everyone who encounters them and is willing to hear.

# *"It never, ever was easy, but it was always, always right."*

## Interview with Janice Fialka

*By Mark Larson (2012)*

### Introduction

*Janice conducts workshops for schools, human service organizations, and parent and advocacy groups on the challenges and possibilities facing parents and professionals as they seek to build successful working relationships on behalf of children with disabilities.*

*Her husband, Richard Feldman, is a former autoworker and longtime community and labor activist. Their daughter, Emma Fialka-Feldman, 23, is studying to be a special education teacher in Boston.*

*Their son, Micah Fialka-Feldman, 28, has an "intellectual disability" and, in a federal case, fought for his right to live in a dorm while he attended Oakland University. He now works as a peer-to-peer counselor at Syracuse University.*

*In May 2014, Micah was appointed by President Barack Obama to the President's Committee for People with Intellectual Disabilities.*

*Janice talks about Micah's birth and childhood and how she and her family came to expect that Micah be welcomed as a valued member of the community and school, not in spite of his "disability" but because, like everyone, his experience is unique and essential to the whole.*

### *I*

Early on, we knew that Micah would have all these labels attached to him. "Failure to thrive," then "developmentally delayed." When he was born, he had an Apgar score of 4, then 7, I think, which isn't terribly horrible. But he was rushed to an ICU. The beginning was pretty traumatic for a new mom who was a somewhat competent social worker, working with teen moms. And all of a sudden she has her own child who wasn't very responsive and was incredibly colicky. I couldn't stop his crying. He didn't nurse, which is so primal to who you are as a mother. I was of the feminist generation, so I never thought about bottle feeding my child. It was like a mortal sin, you know? That really shattered my sense of who I am in those early days.

There's this state of anxiety, What's going on? Why is this happening? I mean, now looking back, we can understand it more from a physiological perspective. He had low muscle tone, as they say, so that impacted his ability to nurse. But at the time it felt very psychological and personal. I think that in those early days I was in such shock. Any time I leapt to thoughts of the future it was a moment of sheer panic and anxiety. It was doom and gloom and how could this be happening and this isn't what I want.

Also, I think — this is very controversial to say — but I think eventually I began to feel some shame, you know? Why me? What does this say about me in terms of my identity of who I am, that I couldn't give birth to a typical child? And shame is a hard one to get over. Now, the good news is that I've launched myself far away from that. We move past it. But we're able to leave it quicker when we can acknowledge it and have people around us who validate and acknowledge it, too.

***How did you see yourself getting through this?***

I think that eventually I just began to ask for help. And certainly this has been the story of Micah's life. One of the subtitles of his story could be, "learning to ask for help and reaching out to the community." When he was about 14 months, we began the path of intervention. Not unlike a lot of parents, we wanted to do everything possible so that he could be "normal." You want to do everything possible to build on the strengths of the child and intervene so that they can have a fighting chance. I think it comes out of a perspective of, certainly, love, but also this idealized version of what it means to be "normal." That's the journey that Micah has taken us on.

## II

Early on he was in a neighborhood program. A friend of ours in the city ran a beautiful school out of her home where she had chickens and a garden. Rather than doing the typical school plays, they enacted Rosa Parks sitting down on the bus. They took turns being Rosa Parks and the police officer. So that was a very enriching environment and fit with our own personal values of social justice. So he was fully included in that setting.

Then he started first grade. He was in what was then called the "opportunity room," which basically was a room for kids with disabilities, so it was what I would have then called a "self-contained classroom." They were well-meaning folks, but Micah came home one day and said, "I want to go in the same door as all my other friends." That really opened up our eyes. And these were the heydays, the mid-80's, for this whole movement about full inclusion. So we benefited from that and went to a lot of workshops and learned about Circle of Friends, modifications and accommodations and realized that with the right support, Micah could be in general education classes and thrive and be with his peers.

So the concept of being fully included became our goal. It never, ever was easy, but it was always, always right. Not that we didn't have doubts and worries. Depending on how you look at him, through what lens, you either see ability or you see deficiency. He can't make change for a dollar, say. He can't read.

He can't read. He does use technology and speaks into the software program and it comes out in text. That's the strength of technology.

When Micah was in late elementary, Richie kept saying, "This is what we've got to do. We got to work on his computer skill." Rich pushed that, and that is really what saved Micah or gave him many opportunities, because he could communicate that way.

He may not learn the entire curriculum, but we always tried to focus on two or three elements per unit. So he was always with his peers, which we thought made a whole lot more sense, especially in those early years when language was a bit challenging for him. We never could understand why you would put him in a language-delayed classroom. You'd much rather want him in an environment where there were rich conversations going on.

Here's an example: Richie was, still is, very active in a lot of political organizations. So Micah always went to political gatherings. When he was eight days old, just out of the NICU [Neonatal Intensive Care Unit], the first thing he did was go to an anti-nuclear rally. [Laughs] Every week, Richie had some place to go to in particular. One day, Richie went up to get Micah from his bedroom and Micah had his stuffed animals and toys in a circle. Richie said, "What are you doing?" Micah said, "I'm playing Meeting."

So that's what I mean about opportunities. Recently, I was able to find the psych testing that was done when he was eleven and a half years old, and his IQ was 40. So imagine if we would have believed, if you will, in that number.

But on the other side, it's easy to lose being the mother and move into being the therapist. It was getting to the point where all this therapy and intervention was really taking my child away from me. I secretly said, "I'm not going to do any of the therapy they tell me for this summer, and I'm just going to go to kids' music concerts, every single one I can find, and we're going to have fun together." And that's the summer I fell back in love with my son, because I stopped being his interventionist and moved more into mothering.

## III

***This struggle for inclusion, is it about him as an individual, or is about something larger?***

Yes, larger, absolutely. I don't know how people who weren't raised in the 60's do this. [Laughs]. I'm being facetious, but if you talk to other parents, many of them become activists in some way. They begin to see that this is about a social justice issue. I've always said that being part of the woman's movement was so transformative for me, because I learned the personal was political. Disabilities is often seen as a special ed issue rather than a social justice issue. We didn't see it that way right at the beginning. But over time, because of marvelous people, we learned that Micah has a right; morally, we need to include him as a person.

***Who are you today because of Micah?***

[Pause] You just went right to my heart. I still struggle with, "Am I okay?" But he's taught me, in such a deep way, that there's so many ways to be in this world. He's taught me that the only way to get through it is to build a circle of support, to build a community, to ask for help, to invite help. I mean, that's how we've gotten through this. I think the panic in the early years was not only, "Am I good enough?" It's, "Can I survive this?" I feel like, in so many ways, we are very, very blessed with a deep way of being in the world because of him.

We learned that disability is a cultural experience. It's an ethnicity, if you will. And we didn't grow up in that world, so we went to disabled activists, and said, "Teach us what we need to know." So my world is broader and bigger than it ever would have been if Micah was born "typical." I found a voice. I found my voice. My simple stories over the years have been helpful to other families. That's a gift that totally surprised me. I've learned that part of life is very, very hard. It just is. But to know people who have said no to discrimination, who have said "I belong; I matter; there's not one way of contributing in this world, I can contribute," is riches that go beyond gold. As schmaltzy as that might sound, it's very real.

***What do you want teachers to know?***

That their greatest gift, their greatest tool is to listen. It requires that teachers come to a total stop to be with us, not leap to immediate fix-it solutions, but try to understand more about the strengths of that family and what that family perceives and needs. Along with that listening comes the validation of our experiences and our feelings. So that's one thing.

Another is to see the magic in each child. If they can't see it right away, find other people who will help them see it. Because every kid can do something. Every kid. I say to teachers, "Take away the word 'expert' and in its place put the word, 'contributor.' Because everybody can contribute something to understanding that child."

I think that the final thing is to celebrate. Micah's fourth grade teacher lived across the street and she called late one night and said, "I never call parents this way, but I can tell that all your lights are on, and before I went to bed, I just wanted you to know that Micah counted to 30 today." And that's all I needed to know for weeks and weeks! He counted to 30!

***What do you imagine Micah will do with his life?***

I think he has a role to teach, to share his story, to be kind; his kindness can be a skill. How the world will help him do that and open doors to him still looms large as a worry at times. I think he could work in the university. Be sort of a TA for various classes and tell his story so that people can see that people with these differences can participate in these ways. It's so clear to me that that could happen because of the way he changes people's perceptions.

When he was in Syracuse a year ago to do a keynote at this conference, he called me on the fourth day, and he said, "Mom, this is the next door I want to open."

## EPILOGUE

***What do you identify as the Goliath he and we will face?***

A misunderstanding of what it means to be human. Overadherence to so-called perfection, of one way of being, one way of thinking. The over-infatuation with testing. Not seeing the abilities and opportunities, the gifts.

***What do you see as your slingshot?***

That metaphor is a hard one, because it reeks of violence. [Laughs]

***But it's just a pebble.***

OK, a pebble. Definitely perseverance. Unrelenting perseverance. Not doing it alone, reaching out to others, asking, and inviting people to join us in this, help us. Realistically, learning to have fun in the face of the harder times. That really is important. We can become so serious, so driven, and I'm not saying I'm good at this all the time, but I have learned that I better have fun and my kids better have fun.

# *"A community that does not include all of its members is not a community at all."*

## Interview with Micah Fialka-Feldman

*By Mark Larson (2012)*

### Introduction

***In 2003, Micah and several other students with intellectual disabilities began sitting in on regular classes at Oakland University (OU) through a Transition Program sponsored by a local school district, in collaboration with the university. During the next few years, Micah took two buses to the campus each day, attended classes, actively participated in student organizations and extracurricular activities, volunteered in the Student Activities Center and the childcare center, and was known as a "OU student." In 2007, the university initiated a new program called OPTIONS which allowed Micah and other students to continue learning as students at OU.***

***In May 2014, Micah was appointed by President Barack Obama to the Committee for People with Intellectual Disabilities.***

***Micah tells me about the trial that challenged Oakland University's refusal to allow him to live in a dorm like other students.***

### *I*

I was going to school at Oakland University. When I went in to pay tuition, I said I could live in the dorm. They said I could live in the dorm and I applied, and they took my money. Then the vice president, who's a very nice vice president, she just said no. I couldn't live in the dorm because one of their policies they came up with was that I had to be toward a major, toward a degree. But I was paying the same amount of money as anyone else and taking 12 credits. They said I could live in the dorm, but then said no.

***How did you find out?***

I got three letters. So I set up a meeting with the vice president all on my own. I tried to tell her that I was very capable, and I traveled a lot and I was very capable of living in the dorm. They said no.

***Did they give a reason?***

Yeah, they kind of gave a couple reasons. They were kind of not reasons that I believed. They said I wouldn't know how to leave during a fire drill, and that friends in the dorms wouldn't know how to be friends with me and stuff.

***How did you respond to that?***

I was upset and sad, because I probably have more friends than the vice president and most of the people that work at the university.

***So they had a wrong idea about you?***

Yeah. I kind of took the next step of trying to go to my school's board of trustees, and I tried to explain to them that I was very capable. I thought because they were the board of trustees, I thought they would overturn the ruling, but no, they followed what the vice president said.

But the cool thing is, after we found out, I had a friend that was in my fraternity. I had joined a community service fraternity, and I had a friend that was living in the apartment close to campus. I lived there every Tuesday night. It was very cool. I could live away from my parents and stuff. That was cool. My housing case took two years. I was living with my friend some of the time, in his apartment, then I was living at home some of the time.

***What was the hearing like?***

In my lifetime, I never thought I would have a lawyer, but I had a lawyer. He was a great lawyer, Chris Davis. He and

I learned a lot. It was through the Michigan Protection and Advocacy. It's an agency that helps people who have disabilities. It doesn't cost money. They work through the state. I was questioned for five hours in a room.

***By whom?***

There was their lawyer and then there was a lawyer that they kind of hired from some big law firm.

***It sounds like their argument was that you did not have the ability to live there.***

Yeah, that was their big thing. Every month we would go to the board of trustees and we would meet. Meet them and try to explain to them. Many people came and spoke at the meetings saying I can do stuff. We got notes sent to them saying that I was capable of living there, and we hoped that they would make the decision then. It was in 2008 that we went back to the board. We thought they would overturn the ruling, but they followed what the school said. I told them I could live there as a test and try it out and see how it goes. Things like that. But no. They kept it going.

***So you actually went to trial.***

Yeah. It was like a last resort. I was hoping that they would just move on and be happy and say ok.

***Were you nervous about it?***

No, I wasn't nervous. I was very pleased. I knew that I was on the right side. I knew that I was very capable of living in the dorm.

***II***

***In my previous conversation with Micah's mother, Janice, she said: "Five hours of deposition. They put the vice president right across the table from him; they put a video camera on him. Five hours. When it is over, he gets in the car; I was wait-***

***ing. I want to know everything about it, but I'm practicing being a good mother, and I keep my mouth shut. I just ask the question, 'So, how you doing?' He goes, 'The very last question they asked me, Mom, was, Do you think the vice president is discriminating against me because of my disability?' And I told them, 'Yes.' Then Micah turns to me, and he says, "Do you think I hurt her feelings?"***

***When did you learn about the decision?***

The decision was made January of 2010. I was in Florida on vacation. Out with my family and seeing my grandma. It was cool that I found out with my grandma. I got a phone call. It was my lawyer. He said, "I just heard that you won." I said "Oh, that's cool." He explained what we had to do. Things like that. We were worried that they were going to try to appeal. They *kind* of appealed, but they didn't win the appeal somehow during the appeal process.

***What was it like when you entered the dorm for the first time?***

Yeah, it was cool, spending the first night there. I had lunch and dinner with people on my floor. It was fun being in the dorm room, but I had to fight for two years just to live in a small little dorm room. [Laughs]

***Why do you think the school fought so hard against your request?***

Why I think they fought so hard is because they were trying to show that they were right. They were trying to show that they knew that they were right, they were the right people to win. But I'm not sure why they fought so hard. I was capable of living in the dorm, I think. They wasted tons of cash and money on that. The sad thing and the unfortunate thing after I won and after I graduated, a couple of months after that, they unfortunately closed the program I was in. Before I left, I gave the vice president a poster, my famous quote I like: "A community that does not accept all of its members is not a community at all," and I do like that quote a lot.

***Have you had any conversations with her since the decision?***

She was nice when I came by her office before I was heading out to graduate. She was nice. In a couple years from now, I would like to meet with her and see why she really did it. I don't know. I would like to meet with her in a couple years just to see what her ways of thinking, why she really spent all this money and time and stuff. I was home visiting this summer, but I didn't stop by her office. I haven't seen her that much

***How did you feel about the people who didn't want you living in the dorm?***

Some days it was easy, and some days it was hard to do a case. I knew in my heart that I was not doing it for me but I was doing it for other people that would come right after me.

***III***

***Janice: "It baffled him. Not unlike any of us might, he took it personally. He'd say to me, 'Why doesn't the vice president understand that I can take the bus and that I can do all these things, Mom?' And I'd say to him, 'Micah, you know people weren't upset with just Rosa Parks sitting down on the bus. They could take one Rosa Parks. They just didn't want all African-Americans sitting on the bus and going to schools and having the equal rights. It's about who comes after Rosa Parks."***

***When you give these talks across the country about your experiences, Micah, what do you want people to know?***

I want them to know that people who have disabilities have dreams and if they have a good team and a good family, they can get support from their family and stuff. I want people to understand that people with disabilities have dreams and can believe in their dreams.

***You sound very fair and very open-minded to me.***

It's just how I've grown up.

## POST-SCRIPT

***A year before we talked, Micah was asked to keynote at the "disAbled and Proud" conference at Syracuse University which led to his present position there. "I was impressed by the work they've been doing in disability work and all kinds of work. Inclusion and stuff. After being there, I thought of like moving here and stuff. I thought of moving there, because they've been doing work on disability for the last 40 years. I just thought, I love living in Michigan; I lived there my whole life. But I just thought of trying something new."***

***In 2014, President Barack Obama appointed Micah to the President's Committee for People with Intellectual Disabilities.***

# *"I decided I wanted to be a teacher because I wanted other siblings to see that their brother or sister is valued in a school."*

## Interview with Emma Fialka-Feldman

*by Mark Larson (2012)*

### Introduction

***When I first talked with Emma, she was in the midst of her training at the Boston Teacher Residency program. She talked with me about growing up with a brother, Micah, who has an "intellectual disability," how he fought in court for his right to live in a dorm, and how their life together affected her decision to become an educator.***

### Emma's Prologue

I'm in the very beginning phases of becoming a teacher. I just moved to Boston in July after spending a year doing service learning, social justice, leadership workshops and international volunteer tours on the U.S. / Mexico border. I graduated from Mt. Holyoke a year ago with a major in critical social thought. I also had a licensure in early childhood education.

I was looking at the role that fear plays in creating policy, particularly on immigration issues and education. Then I did my capstone paper on how disability will challenge us to redefine humanness if we want to see disability valued in our world, in our society. And that means we have to redefine how we define life, how we define what learning looks like. When I think about my brother's experience, I think about how he's been able to value himself, and what expectations have changed and shifted as a result of that.

*I*

***How much do you think Micah and your being his sister impacted your career choice?***

I think 110%. There are two things that really influenced me wanting to go work with kids. One, I did really well in school. My mom likes to quote my first grade teacher who said that "school was made for Emma and Emma was made for school." I knew how to negotiate that. Most of my friends did not like school and that frustrated me. Not because I wanted them to like school, but because I felt like if we're going to spend so much time in school, how come what was not working for my friends was working for me? Why didn't they have the same rush when they got a paper assignment that I did? What was different about the school experience for them than for me?

I wanted school to be a place where all kids wanted to be. So that was part of it. Then I also saw how inclusion was essential to not only my brother's experience but to all of his friends' experience, all of his non-disabled friends. How much people grew and how our community shifted and how our family was changed by that. I wanted to help make inclusive classrooms really work. I knew that they only worked for Micah, in many ways, because my parents fought so hard to make them work well. My brother's experience of inclusion should not be unique.

***Do you have an early memory of becoming aware of his disability as a child?***

The only reason I know this story is because my mom shares it with me. I don't know if I really remember it. The only time my brother and I ever went to the same school was when I was in first grade, and he was in fifth grade. Micah always had friends around him during recess. That would be the only time I'd really see him. Then second grade, I was in the bathroom with my mom, and I said, "Why does Micah go ah-ah-ah?" I was getting at, why does he stutter? And I also was asking, "Why can't Micah read?"

My mom said she remembers feeling so vulnerable and so scared to answer this question, because it was really the first time I was bringing up this difference I was noticing. She said, "You know how your grandma uses a cane? Well, Micah needs supports just like your grandma uses a cane, so he has extra people to help him with reading." Then I was like, "Okay." I was fine. My mom was waiting for 10 other questions, but that was all I needed at that moment. There was no labeling, it was just, that was what it was.

I think I'm the luckiest kid to have had the parents I've had. They worked really hard to listen to me. I think when you have your kid tell you they don't want your brother and the parent just is like, "Okay," I think that's very magical. That they can listen and not put judgment on what I'm saying and not think I'm a bad kid and just think, "This is just how Emma's feeling at this moment." And I know because my parents have told me, they never knew what our relationship would look like. Now, when my brother and I are back home and we're interacting and we make fun of our parents and we roll our eyes when they talk, all the things that parents want their kids to do, I think they feel satisfied. They figured out how to make it work in our family.

Doesn't mean it was always easy, though. I didn't like my brother all the time. Particularly in middle school, I wished that he wasn't disabled. I tried to fix him. There were a lot of different stages I went through, and I still go through them. Sometimes he's still really embarrassing; I can still get embarrassed that he stutters or takes a longer time to do things.

***So what does that do to the Emma the professional, when Emma the sister starts having that feeling?***

I decide I want to be a teacher because I want other siblings to see that their brother or sister is valued in a school. If there's one reason why I want to do inclusion, it's because I want the siblings, the other Emmas to know that their brother or sister has friends, real friends, not just the random buddy programs.

***So it's not just for the other Micahs. It's for the other Emmas, too.***

Right, exactly. In order to incorporate disability as something that's human, things have to shift in a way that I think is fundamental in how we structure our societies. How we think about what life looks like. Life is so tied to how we think of what is human, how you live your life. Our humanness is also tied to whether you're able to do well in school, how you learn, and my brother has challenged me to think differently about how people learn. Again, schools don't work for everyone, and I'm sure all the people you've been talking to know that. I think disability challenges us to look at what values we put in the school system and what values aren't in there.

***II***

***Describe the teacher you want to become.***

I don't want to be a teacher that forms kids. I know that kids will influence me and I'll influence kids. But I don't want to make kids into something that they're not supposed to be or don't want to be. But I do want to make more Micahs.

***What is a "Micah"?***

I want more kids, particularly kids with intellectual disabilities, and kids with more significant disabilities, to know that they're disabled and are okay with being disabled and know that there's a history of what it means, there's a culture and history around disability. To have incredible supports that let them take risks. I think that often, disabled kids, particularly those with intellectual disabilities, don't get to take risks. We keep them safe because we think that safety is about not taking risks. But Micah has become more safe because his community has grown as a result of his taking risks.

I have two minds working when I'm interacting with Micah. I see us being siblings and then also the, not obligation, but I know all this history and all of the stuff that's not right that I am constantly trying to make it right when I'm talking to him.

I'm trying to do all the tips that I've learned that give people with disabilities dignity. It's also the natural way that I interact with my brother, but now I'm analyzing how I'm interacting with him and what forces are affecting my interactions with him.

***Do you worry about him?***

My big worry for him is that people don't challenge him enough. Through his life, will the people who like Micah, and that he feels very safe with, just keep him at that level and not challenge him? I worry about that.

***What doesn't he get about you?***

When I came out as gay, that was confusing for him. Which I think says a lot about the world we live in. Micah being the most open person in the entire world – anyone who has met Micah knows, he's the most accepting person. This internalization about queer being weird and different and not normal is so deep in who we are that even my brother…He'd picked it up, whether he wanted to or not. It doesn't say so much about him, it just says so much about this world and who we value and what we value.

It didn't feel like he respected me. It wasn't so much when I came out as gay as when I told him I had a girlfriend. I didn't feel like he was, respectful is not the right word, but he wasn't excited for me.

He needed someone else to tell him that who I liked was okay. One of his cousins that he really appreciates told him once, like soon after I told him about my girlfriend, he said, "Micah, some people like boys and some people like girls, and that's okay." Then Micah was okay, he was totally fine with it, and he's been wonderful. My girlfriend and he are just magical. That's another whole story, when you have a brother with a disability, finding a partner who gets your family and gets him in a way that is important.

I like when people know my brother, listen to him enough to

be able to describe him with his disability and, also know he's not always a nice person. Like he smiles a lot, but sometimes he's not always a nice person. And that's okay, that's part of inclusion, that's part of community.

***What was going on for you at the time of his trial for the right to live in a dorm?***

I was very far removed from all of it. I was away at college. Micah would forward me whatever article that he got written about him. He gets lots of press. If you walk into his room, he has every article ever written in the newspaper in a beautiful frame. Anyway, I felt removed from it, but then luckily, when they found out about the ruling, we were all together in Florida. I was actually with him when the lawyer called. My parents were out of the hotel room. He smiles and he tells me.

I was like, "We have to call Mom and Dad, but we don't tell them the ruling. I don't want to do it over the phone; I want to see their reaction." So Micah calls our parents, and they come up. He is under the bed so it looks like he's crying, like he's sad. [Laughs] We set them up. They come in and he just gets up right away and he's like, "I'm moving in."

And that's all really nice. If I could pick one moment to be there for, that would be the moment. And I got to help him move in, which was wonderful and reciprocal and how it should be. Micah got to move me in; I got to move him in. It feels fair, it feels right. I think what was hard and really unsettling was reading comments that people wrote after NPR did a story on him. People had the most disgusting things to say. I'd never heard people say such mean things about Micah. They didn't know who he was. They're just random people who blog and write comments. I know it was really hard for my mom. My dad just says it's disgusting and then that's the end of his analysis of it.

But the beautiful thing that came out of it was, there are people in Micah's community who dedicated days to responding to every comment. "Actually," they'd write, "that's not right."

And, "Actually, Micah's not a unique story." How cool is it when there's a bad thing that happens, the community responds by saying, "We're going to back you up, Micah!"

## EPILOGUE

***What would you say is the Goliath you're up against professionally?***

The Goliath I'm up against is that we assume destiny, and we don't give choices and options and opportunities. How do we also give value and dignity to other ways of being? How do we give dignity to all the work that needs to be done in this world? I think I'm up against a value system that values things that I don't think should be valued, or that have too much emphasis. Like independence over interdependence. Help is seen as something that's bad. Slow as something that's bad

***What do you see as your slingshot?***

I think a lot of relationships with people and a lot of listening.

***And that's what you're doing.***

Yeah. I hope so.

## POST-SCRIPT

Emma is now 1st and 2nd grade teacher at Mission Hill School, an inclusive, project-based school in Boston.

# *Open Heart Surgery*

## *HeartWork: Facing Micah's Open Heart Surgery*

*"Hello Mr. and Ms. Fialka-Feldman. This is Dr. Gorman. I just met your son a few hours ago. I am glad we have this chance to talk. Your son has an ascending aorta aneurysm and will need open heart surgery soon."*

Instantly I lost all ability to breathe.

This shattering news was delivered in a phone call from our son Micah's new cardiologist in Syracuse. Micah lives in Syracuse. We live in Michigan. The 300-mile distance between homes suddenly felt like 3 million miles. At that moment, there was only one place I wanted to be – next to our 29 year old son, holding him, holding his heart.

As the physician continued to explain possible next steps, all color drained from our faces. Our bodies commanded a complete shut down, perhaps to avert total disintegration. The cardiologist's explanations hit me like speeding bullets – bullets we desperately wanted to dodge.

We had almost three decades of life-altering news about Micah and his many disabilities. From when he was 18 months and was labeled "neurologically impaired" to the more recent "needs open heart surgery soon." "Not one more" I wanted to scream. This news came out of nowhere – and it was huge. Although we knew Micah had an unusual heart valve, there never was mention of open heart surgery or aneurysm. He appeared healthy and active. His last cardiologist check-up in Detroit, two years ago, warranted, "Come back in **three** years for your next appointment."

Thank goodness Micah decided that because he was no longer living in Michigan, he wanted to have a new heart doctor in Syracuse. This decision may have saved his life.

But on this Friday, no one anticipated this news. No one wanted this news. No one was prepared to deal with this news.

After a long 20-minute conversation (mainly of Rich and me trying to listen to words we didn't want to hear), the cardiologist reassured us that he would be available to talk over the next few days. We concluded the call and took what seemed like our first breath since that initial, "Hello Mr. and Ms. Fialka-Feldman."

After the phone call, our minds raced. *What do we do now? How is Micah? Should we drive to Syracuse immediately? Will he survive? Why is this happening? Who do we talk to? (again) Should we immediately drive to Syracuse? How could we not? What is Micah going through?*

We took another breath, practiced our not-too-worried voices and called Micah. "Hey Micah, how are you doing? You know we just talked to Dr. Gorman and he let us know about your heart. We love you a lot."

Micah's voice was softer than usual but there was no apparent panic. Like us, he was numb to the news.

**Micah:** *"Yah, that was weird. I just went in to meet a new doctor to get a check -up and he tells me I need heart surgery, and on a Friday afternoon."*

**Me:** *"That must have been hard to hear. How are you doing?"*

**Micah:** *"Okay." (Silence.) "I mean it's kinda hard to hear this from someone you don't even know."*

**Me:** *"Yes, it must be really hard, Micah." (Pause.) "Are you with someone now?"*

**Micah:** *"No, just watching the news."*

I imagined Micah sitting all alone on the couch, curled up with a pillow. I longed to be sitting next to him.

**Me:** *"Sometimes when we hear news we didn't expect, it helps to be with a friend or family. Dad and I would be very happy to make a visit tonight or tomorrow if you'd like. You know we love seeing you."*

(I remind myself to keep my voice v-e-r-y calm.)

**Micah:** *"I don't know."*

**Me:** (Trying hard to think of what to say next.) *"Would you like to be with one or two of your friends tonight? Just to hang out. Doesn't have to be anything serious, just to be with someone. Maybe get some ice cream."*

**Micah:** *"Yah, sure."*

(Rich and I look at each other, wondering what is the best thing to do right now? Wouldn't good parents immediately hop in their car and drive to be with their son? Why are we not going? What's right to do?)

**Rich:** *"If you were going to hang out with a friend tonight, who are the top two or three friends you'd like to be with?"*

(Micah shares three names.)

**Rich:** *"Great. Would you like to call them or would you like us to call them?"* (We fall back on one of our guiding parenting principles: "Give Micah choices. Don't make the choice for him.")

**Micah:** *"Yah, you can phone them."*

I hear relief in his voice. He gives us the phone numbers. (Despite our shaking hands, we manage to scribble the numbers on a scrap of paper.)

**Me:** *"Okay, Micah, we'll call them and get right back to you. We love you lots."* (It seems that we can't say that enough at this moment.)

Still fighting back the intense desire to drive to Syracuse, we phone each of Micah's friends and explain the situation. They are eager to support him. They decide that the best thing to do is to call Micah and arrange for a sleepover for tonight. We thank them and remind them to call us right away if we need to do something. We end the call and burst into held-back tears. For a moment we feel some welcome relief knowing that our son won't be alone in his room with heavy thoughts of hospitals, surgery, and scary words he has never heard before. Over the next few days, Micah's Circle of Support, his friends

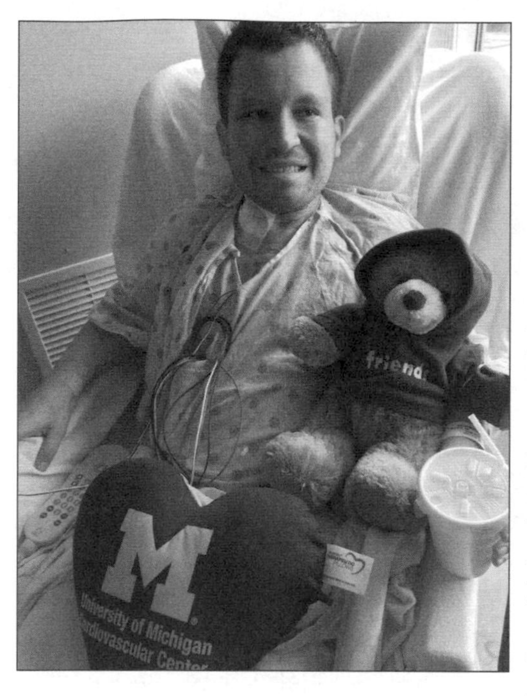


and colleagues, organize a way to support him. They work out where he will spend a few nights, who will talk with him and hang out with him, and who will help Micah keep us posted on how he is handling this news. Rich and I emphasize that we are willing and eager to immediately hop in our car and drive full speed to be with him. "Just let us know and we will come." We let Micah know as well, and talked with him twice a day.

**Are we doing this right?**

During those very long 10 days when Micah was in Syracuse and we were in Michigan, we never, not for a second, stopped worrying or wondering if we should be with Micah in his home. We asked ourselves a million times, "Are we doing the right thing?"

But somehow, all the lessons we had learned over the past 25 years, especially from the disability community, about self-determination, ensuring authentic opportunities for Micah's growth, relying on natural supports and taking risks, were guiding us in how best to handle this delicate and difficult situation. The main two lessons were: "Don't rush to rescue" and "Respect his resiliency."

**The role of Micah's Circle**

Over the past two-and-a-half years, Micah had worked hard to establish a formal and informal Circle of Support who were engaged and involved in his life. They met monthly, as well as informally. If we charged in immediately, it would be much harder for the Circle to be actively engaged with Micah, and for Micah to seek out his supports. With Micah's involvement and agreement, we decided to notify and nudge his community to give them the opportunity to work with Micah on how to live with this news. The participation of his friends strengthened his connections with his circle, and their connections with him.

We also wanted Micah to know that we respect him and his ability to live more *inter*dependently – not totally without us, but with some space between him and us – a welcoming space others are encouraged to inhabit.

In no way did we, or could we, remove ourselves from being intimately involved. Rich drove to Syracuse about 10 days after hearing the news from Dr. Gorman and spent the weekend with Micah, to be with him and to gain a sense of how he was handling the life-changing news. His sister, Emma, drove from Boston to the Massachusetts and New York border to be together with her brother for a few hours.

We worked hard not to be Micah's dominant protectors. If we "took over," we would interfere with his ability to build his decision-making skills, hinder his personal and social growth, and interfere with his resiliency.

Micah remained in Syracuse most of the next two months until his surgery in Michigan. Because of the intense and long recovery, Micah and his Syracuse cardiologist agreed that it was best for him to have the surgery in Michigan. The week before he left Syracuse, his friends and Circle gave him a "going away party." They stayed in touch with gifts, emails, texts, and phone calls over the three months he was recovering in our home.

**Danger and Opportunity for Growth**

The next year-and-a-half were deeply challenging. Micah did well physically during and after the surgery. The aneurysm was repaired and his valve was replaced, but the psychological and physical shock to his body and mind definitely impacted his sense of safety and heightened his anxiety. Many of his Syracuse friends and several compassionate and skilled professionals guided him through this difficult time. In particular, his social worker from University of Michigan Hospital, Leah Brock went beyond the call of duty. She never once stopped supporting Micah with enormous skill, great compassion, hundreds of emails, and massive patience and perseverance. Everyone needs a "Leah" when life hits so hard.

The story of Micah and his heart surgery has many complicated twists and turns. It was by far the hardest experience we faced as a family. As in all crises, there is both danger and opportunity for growth. Our family definitely experienced danger.

**Building Resilience**

Luckily, we all did some growing too. I learned from Micah the power of having my own circle of support. It wasn't easy for me, but I took advice from my son and invited a group of my women friends to be my Circle during the months of his surgery and recovery. At our first gathering, a week before Micah's surgery and three weeks after my dear mother had unexpectedly died, my circle sat in a circle in my friend's cozy living room. Each of us read a quote about courage; each shared a time in our lives that required courage we weren't sure we possessed. Everyone benefitted, reminding me of one of the shared quotes: "Resilience is a shared commodity in that one person generates it in another." Micah's need for open heart surgery was a two-year experiment in generating and re-generating resilience in his community, in our community, and in ourselves.

**Role of Parents: Protectors and Guides**

A sociologist once told me that there are two primary roles that parents can take in raising their children: role of protector and role of guide. During the "Heart Surgery Chapter" of Micah's life, we did some protecting for sure, but overall we practiced (with several bouts of failing!) doing more guiding and creating opportunities for Micah to make decisions with supports.

Our first visit with the renowned heart surgeon in Michigan was tense, despite the staff's care and welcoming spirit. We sat in a sterile exam room, "decorated" with posters and plastic models of the heart. As the surgeon began his explanation of the procedure, I felt Micah's anxiety flood the room.

I swirled in thoughts of, *What do I do? Protect? Guide? Rescue? How do I help?*

Then I remembered one of our family's guiding principles: "Give Micah choices." Awkwardly I interrupted the physician. "I apologize for interrupting, doctor, but I want to check in with Micah right now." Quickly and with all the fake calm I could muster, I offered, "Hey Micah, there is a lot going on here. I am wondering what might be best for you right now. I think there are two choices. You could stay in the exam room with dad and me and listen or you could wait in the waiting room and then dad and I will share everything the doctor said." Without a moment of hesitation, Micah stood up, turned toward the door, and announced, "I'll be in the waiting room."

Micah and his anxiety left the room, only to be replaced with all of our concerns about Micah's ability to handle such a serious surgery. Understandably, the medical team expressed apprehension, and honestly Rich and I were uncertain about Micah's capacity to handle the procedure and recover.

However, Micah and others have taught us is that there is a process to being able to do the hard things. The more Micah could make choices, receive support and have his fears validated, the better. The more he could be encouraged to take small steps, the better equipped he was at handling very difficult situations. It just took a bit longer.

In particular, Rich had a loyal, enduring belief in Micah's resiliency. I leaned on his belief and his shoulders constantly. We all got through this in huge part because of Rich's steadfast belief (and humor).

Over time, Micah was able to be more engaged in the medical exams. His own sense of competence and confidence grew. His community of support strengthened. Soon he was able to be involved in every conversation. When it was difficult, Micah asked to have his social worker, Leah present; what a brilliant way to handle a stressful visit. Who wouldn't want Leah nearby!

**A New Chapter in Micah's Life**

Remnants of Micah's surgery experience remain in his life. It has entered into his storytelling. He references it when people talk about hard times. He knows he will probably need another valve replacement in a decade or so and is planning who will be around to support him. He offers to talk to other people, especially those with an intellectual disability who need open heart surgery. "I can tell them that you can get through it. And you have to get a good social worker and have a circle of friends."

Journalist, Ann Fadiman brilliantly describes parenting as "part ecstasy, part panic." It is hard to remember that both ecstasy and panic exist when the panic part is dominant. But, when others encircle us, we can get through the panic part easier and revel in the ecstasy part more.

Although I would do anything to remove the type of panic Micah and our family had to endure, we did live through heart-work. And I am happy to report, that every once in awhile, just when we need it, we are blessed with some glorious moments of ecstasy. We know we are fortunate.

Micah's heart, which has always been big, is stronger and beats with more confidence.

*Micah and personal trainer, Karl Sterling staying strong*

# Disability Pride Emerges

# How Roger Ebert's Clarity and Courage Helped Me Redefine My Son's Disability

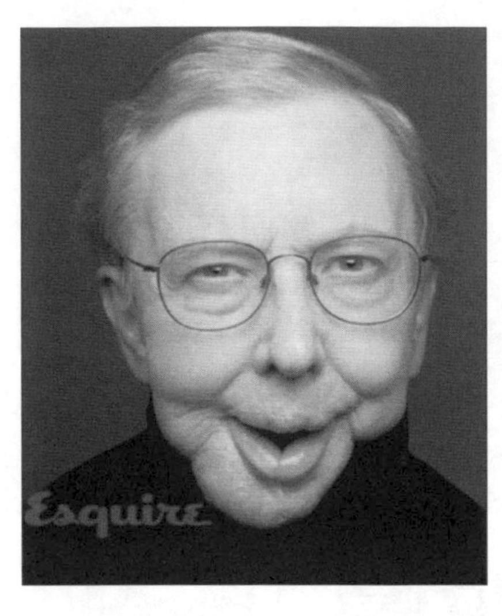


I distinctly remember the moment Roger Ebert became much more than just "my favorite movie reviewer."

I was listening to the radio when the reporter announced that Roger had agreed to grace the cover of the March 2010 Esquire magazine. But this would be no ordinary photo. It would be a full-on shot of his face – without his lower jaw, which had been removed as a result of numerous cancers and surgeries.

No touch ups, no cover ups, no hiding … just as he was. Roger was comfortable with his decision. He wanted folks to know, "This is how I look; this is who I am".

I was moved to tears, not because of what I might see of "my favorite movie reviewer" but because of what I was beginning to see in my own heart.

His decision to show his unusual face spoke loudly to me, the mother of a son with a disability.

This bold sharing was about self-acceptance, dignity and self-respect.

There was no shame or embarrassment, and he invited no pity. Although the cancer had also taken his voice he explained in his stunning 2011 memoir, "Life: Itself", that he was "remaking his voice" and would continue to communicate, just in a different way.

*Originally published in www.shetroit.com. April 2013. Reprinted with permission.*

*Janice, Micah, Emma, Rich in Maine*

Roger's clarity and courage bolstered my own quest to re-define disability. Since our son Micah's birth in 1984, our family has been dealing with society's – and our own – biases and misconceptions.

Gradually, though, Micah has taught us to understand disability not as a misfortune but as a natural part of the human condition. Not as a flaw to be fixed but rather as a call to respect, celebrate, and support differences.

Because of Micah – and with reminders from that famous movie reviewer – I'm learning to place the words "disability" and "pride" right next to each other.

Roger Ebert understood the necessity of breaking the silence about disability and differences. His memoir and the Esquire cover convey his determination to communicate openly about sometimes-challenging realities. He also understood the necessity of community.

Roger valued how his community expanded as he connected to the disability world. He shared about all the people he was meeting via the internet, including a man who typed his responses to Roger's blogs using one toe and another of his favorite bloggers whose name was "Smart Ass Cripple."

*Chaz and Roger Ebert in earlier and healthier years for him*

Roger adored his wife, Chaz, and acknowledged how important she and her large family were to him. He also valued the transformative power of technology, which allowed him to speak again – in a new way.

Like Roger Ebert, we too are learning the power of breaking the silence, of building community, of asking for help, and using technology. Because Micah does not read or write in a typical sense, technology keeps him connected. (If you need evidence of his strong voice and large network, Facebook him now! … or visit the website that follows his journey.)

I will never forget the first email I received from Micah about 10 years ago. Since he had never before shared his ideas in writing, his email caught me totally off guard. I sat reading the six words on my computer screen over and over. As far as I was concerned, he had written an award-winning essay. It simply read, "Hi mom. This is from Micah."

So in 2010, when I heard that Roger Ebert was proudly putting his face on the cover of Esquire, he became more than my favorite movie reviewer – he was now my teacher, my encourager, my guide and friend in spirit – and why I refer to him simply as Roger. His voice came through loud and clear to me, and hopefully to many others who followed his reviews and writings about life, in and out of the movies.

He said he loved film because it encouraged understanding and empathy for those different from ourselves. By sharing his unusual face, Roger himself demonstrated pride and encouraged empathy and acceptance for all who might act or appear outside the norm.

He didn't start out knowing what he knew when he put his face on the cover of Esquire. That kind of wisdom takes time, soul searching, and lots of support. Eventually, though, he arrived at a deep understanding of what was most important in life, and it had nothing to do with the shape of his face or the sound of his voice. As he said in his memoir,

> I believe that if, at the end of it all, according to our abilities, we have done something to make others a little happier, and something to make ourselves a little happier, that is about the best we can do. To make others less happy is a crime. To make ourselves unhappy is where all crime starts. We must try to contribute joy to the world. That is true no matter what our problems, our health, our circumstances. We must try. I didn't always know this, and am happy I lived long enough to find it out.

Roger Ebert loved Leonard Cohen's song, "I'm Your Man." He said it often saved his life.

So to you, Roger Ebert, I sing out in voice, in whispers, in shouts, in grunts, in American Sign Language, in voice technology . . . . "You ARE my man, and my teacher too."

*Thank you to Becca Williams for her strong encouragement and editing.*

## From Puddles to PRIDE

(For all those who marched at the Disability Pride Parade)

When they first gave me the news my child
had a disability
and would forever have a label glued to his name

I discovered sounds in my throat I never knew existed
wails
groans
sobs

Even silent screams
erupted from my throat,
shattered the windows
in my once-called normal home.

After my body emptied
of all sounds
the tears came
madly,

streaming down my cheeks,
sliding down my arms that clutched my baby
raining over my heart.
into puddles,

Puddles all around me
Puddles everywhere
Puddles I thought I would drown in.

That was 19 years ago.

Today, July 18, 2004 on a balmy summer day
in the city of Chicago

I stand

on this street where there are no puddles.

On this street there are feet
of every size, shape, age, and color marching,
    shuffling, rolling
in the first-ever Disability PRIDE Parade.
Yes, I said: Disability Pride Parade!

On this street there are wheels rolling
lovely legs limping
clenched fists raised high
in the cloud-studded blue sky,
beautiful bent smiles exploding with joy.
On this street there are voices, mumbles, grunts, spit,
    hands moving in the air,
shouting out, signing out, singing out:
What do we want?

Accessibility!
When do we want it?
Now!

On this street are people who will
no longer be shunned, excluded,
no longer be segregated, pitied
no longer be tolerated only on
holidays and at charity balls.

On this street is Marlin, regal in his body and chair
singing James Brown with a twist:
"Say it LOUD, I'm Disabled and Proud"
Rallying all young disabled activists to say it, shout it,
sign it and Braille it . . . in all caps, he adds.

On this street is Naomi,
with her
60s-take-to-the-street attitude, shouting,
"We are getting on your agenda."

On this street is our son, Micah
whose label is not a source of shame to him.
Who says, "I meet the best people in the world."

On this street, I look around,
turn to another mother who knows about puddles
and say: "This is how life should look every day,
on every street."

On this street there are no puddles ---
no puddles of shame.
The glorious sunlight has dried them up.

On this street there are no puddles,

There is only PRIDE.
There is only PRIDE.
There is only PRIDE.

*Listen to Janice read this poem, accompanied by music and photos at http://www.broadreachtraining.com/videos/puddles_pride.htm*

*Justin D'artists of Detroit's Matrix Theatre Company (www.matrixtheatre.org)*
*Micah's Dad was often inside the Justin Dart puppet.*

*Jack Pearpoint and Micah*

# Micah and his friends from Inclusion Press

*photo by Franziska Trauttmansdorff*

*Just hanging with my friend Judith Snow*

*Rich, Micah, Janice, Lynda, Jack in Syracuse for Micah's MAP*

# Afterword
# Thoughts from Dad!

*Photo by Sarah Wentworth*

I have had the honor and privilege, as well as stress, pain, fear, uncertainty and confusion of fatherhood since Micah was born in 1984. Through Micah's resilience and spirit, our family has been given the opportunity to make a small contribution to the "understanding that all of us long for inter-dependence -- not independence; community -- not isolation; and education for the heart and hand, not just of the head."

All of it has been a tremendous gift. Though Micah's story is impressive, I am proud of our family's journey, of Micah's courage, Janice's dedication, and Emma's self-understanding and the deep thinking. Micah's younger sister, now a second grade teacher who deals daily with issues of education and inclusion, has often said Micah's story is the community's story.

We are proud to be part of a 30-year journey that has seen decades of work from the Inclusion Press, words and wisdom of Judith Snow, and efforts from so many who raise profound questions at this critical moment in the history of our planet:

**What does it mean to be human?**

**What is success?**

**Where are we going?**

**What are the values that need to guide us as we walk the journey of life, with family, neighbors, as local and global citizens?**

Philosopher-activists and authors, Grace Lee and James Boggs were part of our extended Detroit family, as well as our mentors and dear friends. Our family brought them to the inclusion and the disability justice movement. When Micah was attending Oakland University, Grace and Micah spoke at an inclusive education conference at Wayne State University. Grace's opening remarks began with:

> *Martin Luther King Jr. said that love is not some sentimental weakness, but somehow the key to ultimate reality. Just think about that … how divided our society has become, how separate we are from one another, how competitive we are forced to become, and realize how much we need that kind of heart and relationships. Micah shows us education of the heart. When I think of Micah over the years, he often would say that he goes to meetings to change the world.*

Micah's presence teaches us to ask questions which change the world: **"Who is not at the table? How do we break our own silence and the silence of others?"**

These questions are not abstract. We recognize that we have advantages that supported many of the choices we have made. Janice, who had been a leader in teen sexuality and the health field was able to create a new "career" in thinking, writing, and organizing around disabilities, parent-professinal relationships, advocacy and inclusion. I had the support and benefits of the United Auto Workers Union (UAW), first as an assembly line worker, then as part of the union leadership. Even before the enactment of the Family Medical Leave Act, I could take time to attend meetings, and take Micah to therapy. We were surrounded by loving and caring family and friends. We also had important political experiences in the 1960s that shaped and guided our choices.

Micah was raised with the principles and dreams of great expectations, and the belief that every individual has the right and the responsibility to find his or her passion and make life's journey a path to discovery and meaning.

Janice and I are not naive. We have always been clear that Micah did not face discrimination because of race or gender. When Micah rode the bus for almost two hours for thirty miles from our home to Oakland University, we had less fear about his safety because he was a young white man and not a young woman or a person of color.

Micah's discrimination was around ableism and a system that historically has never addressed the value of human beings and human potential. The gifts everyone brings to his or her family, neighborhood, community, or society are often neglected and seldom honored.

We knew that the "system" would not provide most, if any security. We understood that Micah's future was not separate from our collective ability to create sustainable and loving communities. Our greatest privileges were the critical connections that encouraged us to listen and learn from individuals who committed themselves to creating a future in which "all means all." We have learned "another world is possible" when our imaginations are rich enough. As a family we chose to embrace these concepts. They became our mission and our responsibility.

Through the years, we watched Micah grow and move through multiple obstacles, both the physical doors of discrimination and the walls maintained by insensitivity, ignorance, and bias. His resilience and spirit do open doors, certainly, but those doors don't open nor the walls come down without the sustained efforts of his family, neighbors, peers, professionals, social justice activists, and community who love, support, and surround him. Micah is a magnet for people who want to be part of "what is possible."

Our daughter, Emma introduced us to the idea that, "It not only takes a village to raise a child, it takes a child to raise a village." I have often been amazed at Micah's ability to create circles of support where everyone gives and receives. Dan Wilkins' statement has guided our family over the years, "A Community that excludes even one of its members is no community at all."

When Micah's federal court victory gave him the legal right to live in the dormitory at Oakland University, Bob Williams, current Deputy Commissioner for the Administration on Disabilities and director of the Independent Living Administration, described his reaction this way:

> ***"(W)hen ...I heard the San Francisco sit in succeeded forcing Carter and Califano to enforce Section 504... a rush of pride, tears and joy swept over me that day. Those same feelings of absolute certainty and hope have enveloped me three other times since then:***
>
> 1. ***The day Senator Tom Harkin dedicated the final passage of ADA to children with disabilities born that day;***
> 2. ***When Mandela freed all of his fellow South Africans regardless of the hue of their bodies from the crushing bondage of apartheid;***
> 3. ***And most recently, when Micah Fialka-Feldman, a 25-year-old student with an intellectual disability won the right to live in a dorm at Michigan's Oakland University where he is taking classes.***

In 2017, Micah will be one of the individuals profiled in Dan Habib's forthcoming film. (http://www.iod.unh.edu/inclusivecommunities). The documentary film project, tentatively titled *Intelligent Lives*, explores how the segregation of people with intellectual disabilities became the norm, why this segregation is slowly being dismantled, and how some people with intellectual disabilities are blazing a bold new path.

Daily I am reminded of the wisdom of Grace Lee Boggs, who said, "History is never linear, progress is excruciatingly slow and fate is not to be left to chance. We must shape and be ever ready to be shaped by it."

When I introduce Micah at presentations, I say that there are three principles that guide our family and shape our history:

1. Great Expectations
2. Lifelong learning
3. Authentic Relationships and Community

I thank Janice for never taking a breath in this journey, for telling the story of our family and creating the space for our family's journey to be shared. Janice has been the storyteller, poet, visionary and dreamer, the individual focused on the details, the person nudging and linking networks, the seeker finding and creating resources. Janice's poetry gave voice to our feelings, human frailties, vulnerabilities and joys. Her words expressed our family's journey. In this new edition, *What Matters: Reflections on Disability, Community and Love* the additional writings and stories deepen and expand on her 1997 publication. She and others share a journey few would have predicted.

In the early years, we would say that Micah was our teacher and Emma was our healer. Today, we know that both our children are teachers and healers—of each other, of our family, of the community, and of society.

I am a really lucky husband and dad.

Richard Feldman
May 2016

# About the Family

## About the Family

**Janice Fialka**, LMSW, ACSW is a nationally recognized lecturer and author on issues related to disability, parent-professional partnerships, inclusion, and raising a child with disabilities. She is also a parent, a sometime poet, a storyteller, and an award-winning advocate for families and persons with disabilities. Janice has provided the keynote address and workshops at numerous national, state, and local conferences throughout the United States and Canada and conducts trainings for schools, organizations, and parent and advocacy groups. She was named "Social Worker of the Year" in 2007 by the National Association of Social Workers - Michigan Chapter. Janice, her husband and Paul Rossen produced the film, "Through the Same Door: Inclusion Includes College" which documents Micah's experience as a college student. It received the 2006 TASH Image Award. To celebrate the 25th Anniversary of the Americans with Disability Act (ADA) in 2015, Janice and Rich joined the ADA Legacy Tour (http://www.adalegacy.com/ada25/ada-legacy-tour) bringing the gigantic hero puppet of Justin Dart, known as the father of the ADA, to several cities, including Washington D.C.

**Micah Fialka-Feldman** is a national speaker, teacher, and pioneer who fights for disability-pride, justice, and inclusion. He is part of the first wave of adults with intellectual disabilities attending college and has been fully included in school and community throughout his life. In 2009 he won a Federal law suit which affirmed his right to live in the university dorm in Michigan. Micah currently lives in Syracuse, N.Y. where he received a Certificate in Disability Studies from Syracuse University in 2016. He is a Teaching Assistant in the School of Education at Syracuse University. In 2014, Micah was appointed by President Obama to the President's Committee for People with Intellectual Disabilities. He will be featured in a forthcoming (2017) documentary produced by filmmaker Dan Habib (*Including Samuel*) (www.iod.unh.edu/inclusive-communities).

**Emma Fialka Feldman** is an elementary school inclusion teacher in Boston Public Schools. She received her undergraduate degree from Mount Holyoke College where she studied Critical Social Thought and Early-Childhood Education and her Master's Degree from the Boston Teacher Residency Program. She is interested in and presents on inclusive education

practices and the relationship between siblings with and without a disability She blogs at emmaff.blogspot.com.

**Richard Feldman** has been an activist since the 1960's. He retired in 2015 from the United Auto Workers International staff. Prior to this position, he worked at the Ford Truck Plant for 20 years on the line and 10 years as an elected official. He co-edited the book, "End of the Line: Auto Workers and the American Dream" in 1988, one of the first books written by and with auto workers. For over 40 years, Rich has worked with the ideas and organizations emerging from the work of James and Grace Lee Boggs (www.boggscenter.org). He speaks, writes, and organizes in Detroit and across the country where he is committed to creating local sustainable economies and self-governing democracy. Rich takes seriously MLK Jr.'s commitment to creating the "beloved community" and the words of Dan Wilkins, "A community that excludes even one of its members is no community at all."

In 2009, the national organization, Family Voices honored Janice, Rich, Micah and Emma with a "Lifetime Achievement" Award for their work in disability advocacy.

For more information about Janice's
speaking, training and articles,
or to order publications, please visit:
*danceofpartnership.com*

To learn more about Micah's
speaking, articles, and his journey, visit:
*throughthesamedoor.com*

To learn more about Emma's journey, visit:
emmaff.blogspot.com

# Other Publications from Janice Fialka

**Parents & Professionals Partnering for Children with Disabilities: A Dance that Matters**
Janice M. Fialka, Arlene K. Feldman, Karen C. Mikus
Foreword by Ann P. Turnbull

ISBN 978-1-4129-6639-9

Written from both the parent's and the professional's points of view, this book draws upon the metaphor of dance to highlight the essential partnerhsip between teachers, administrators, support staff, and parents of children with disabilities. Rich with humor and heart, the book offers helpful steps for self reflection, personnel preparation, and parent-professional training.

Published by: Corwin: www.corwin.com

## From Puddles to PRIDE

**A mother's poems about her Son, his Disability, and her Family's Transformation**

On this CD, Janice reads three of her poems, accompanied by original piano music and a stunning presentation of photos and graphics. Two of the poems are from *What Matters: Reflections on Disability, Community and Love.*

ISBN 1-882792-85-8

## Whose Life is it Anyway?

**How one Teenager, her Parents, and her Teacher view the Transition Process for a Young Person with Disabilities**

*Co-authored with Martha Mock and Jennifer Wagner Neugart in collaboration with the Waisman Center at the University of Wisconsin*

This book provides insights into what youth, parents, and professionals experience as they plan for post-high school transition. It encourages the reader to think "outside the box."

## Through the Same Door:

***Inclusion Includes College***

This film documents the fully inclusive education of Micah on a college campus. It received the 2006 TASH Image Award for the Positive Portrayal of People with Disabilities.

ISBN 0-9791903-0-4

# Recent Additions from Inclusion Press

## Resources to Support Your Work & Life

inclusion.com BOOKS • WORKSHOPS • MEDIA • RESOURCES

## *What people say about this book...*

Janice Fialka has taken up the adventure of parenting bravely, creatively, and mindfully, and here she shares a lifetime's harvest of wisdom and practical guidance for families, educators, clinicians, and all the rest of us. She writes, early on, that "Micah has deepened my understanding of the absolute brilliance of asking for help. He is at ease with what he can do and what supports he needs." This is a counter-cultural brilliance in American life, but with a winsome combination of poetry and pragmatism, she reveals it as possible for us all - and as a beautiful way out of the impoverishing illusions of "self-sufficiency" and "normalcy. I am grateful that this mind-opening, life-altering, soul-stretching book is in the world.

*—Krista Tippett, Executive Creator/Host, On Being + The Civil Conversations Project Author, Becoming Wise: An Inquiry into the Mystery and Art of Living*

Take into your heart the message embodied in this book and everything else about inclusive education will naturally fall into place. If you read only one book this year, make it this one. It's the real deal.

*—Cheryl M. Jorgensen, PhD, Inclusive Education Consultant*

Wisdom is timeless, but insight may grow over the years. I am grateful to Janice Fialka for taking the time to reflect on the wisdom she gained as Micah's and Emma's mother, and how her insights have grown in 20 years since her first book. Parents of people with developmental disabilities seldom have time to reflect. *What Matters: Reflections on disability, community and love* is a gift to us, a chance to open our hearts and minds to reflect on our own paths, insights, and wisdom. It is a gift to the field, as well, an invitation to think of how much has changed and how our professional allies have helped to open the horizons for all us. We are in this together.

*—Sue Swenson, Acting Assistant Secretary for Special Education and Rehabilitative Services, US Dept. of Education*

The Fialka-Feldman family has taught me that there can by no inclusion without the inclusion of my son's voice. With Janice's help I have learned that my son's voice is crucial to creating a circle of support. When we listen to him, we learn how to think out of the box; he learns that he belongs at the table both at school and in life. Thank you Fialka-Feldman family for reminding how to listen with love and how to keep dancing when I don't do it so well.

*-Cindy Estrada, Vice President, United AutoWorkers (UAW)*

This book offers delight, clarity and insight not only for those seeking inclusion in society, but for all people working to change things that matter to us. Whatever our cause, the questions persist: How do we persevere for the long term without being overtaken by anger and exhaustion? How do we keep improving relationships with everyone, even those bureaucrats and professionals who hide behind their expertise? How do we celebrate and cry together and learn that joy is always available in our deep connectedness, no matter the external circumstances? These questions are answered here, by this persevering, insightful, loving family and their friends.

*Margaret Wheatley,*
*author of Leadership and the New Science and many other books*

Having a child with a disability makes life busier, more complicated, and much, much more creative. This collection of writings by Janice Fialka, her family, and others captures the evolution of their lives over three decades — lives of adventure, love, laughter and risk taking. With powerful honesty and eloquence, her writing shows us what it means to be fully inclusive, and what it means to be fully human. This collection is an essential toolbox for families and educators who are navigating a world of diverse abilities.

*—Dan Habib, Filmmaker of "Including Samuel" and an upcoming film featuring Micah Fialka-Feldman*

I have always believed that we are all one another's mentors just as surely as we are all one another's mentees. You will see this principle exemplified in Janice Fialka's life and her work which are inextricably intertwined. She has a way of opening her life experience like a book from which we all can benefit and to which we can be contributors. This is an act of great generosity and humility that she has clearly imparted to her children and they, in turn, to us. We learn from them, both about what inclusion really is and also how to draw on and share one's own experiences as an example. I have no doubt that, as a reader, you will find comfort and insight in the warm company of Janice, Rich, Micah and Emma and their friends as soon as you open these pages.

*-Mark Larson, Ed.D*

The webs we weave in our lives can become complex and difficult, especially for families who experience disability (which, ultimately, is likely to be most of us). Janice Fialka reminds us that if we focus upon what is important – love and laughter, creativity and intention, interdependence and community – we can live incredibly rich lives of joy, celebrate difference and move beyond those societal attitudes that can be disabling.

*Sharon Lewis, Former Commissioner*
*Administration on Intellectual and Developmental Disabilities*
*U.S. Dept of Health and Human Services*

I devoured this book in one sitting complete with both laughter and tears. Janice and her family share their stories with an authenticity that is rare but desperately needed in a world that glorifies easy answers, exceptionalism and professional interventions. Through their stories we see that only when we turn towards one another and do what is right, especially when it's hard, do possibilities for a full life truly emerge.

*Caitlin Petrakis Childs, Community Organizer and Consultant Former Director of the Real Communities Initiative.*

You will notice that all of the contributions from others in this book mention friendship. This is not an accident. Janice has many gifts. But most salient is her authentic and intentional ability to truly connect with people. Janice is eager to know.... really know.... YOU. This beautiful give and take is what readers will feel with every entry in this book, old and new. This wonderful compilation invites you into an ongoing conversation about family, disability, hope, and expectation. It asks us to explore important questions about how we can make things better for our families and our communities. This book is a warm hug of encouragement, a shoulder to cry on, a magic mirror that tells each reader in no uncertain terms, "You are not alone!". It will become a touchstone and friend that you can count on for years to come. Just like Janice.

*-Meg Grigal Ph.D, Co-Director, Think College Research Fellow Institute for Community Inclusion, University of Massachusetts Bos***ton**

Janice Fialka chronicles her family's odyssey through challenges and obstacles, false turns and foul winds as they make their way, step by step, with heart and courage and gathering wisdom. What Matters is also a reflection on our wild and dazzling diversity, and the universal and irrepressible agency that lives inside every soul, ready to spark up and surprise us if we're prepared to pay attention, and then fan those first flashes into life-giving fires. This is a book for parents and teachers, lawmakers and policy people, and anyone interested in creating a future fit for all— a place of joy and justice, powered by love.

*-William Ayers, Distinguished Professor of Education (retired), University of Illinois, Best Selling Author:Teaching with Conscience in an Imperfect World*

Nothing sharpens and redefines your priorities as a parent like learning that your child will live with a disability. Typical stresses are quickly forgotten, and new worries can seem insurmountable. In this book of essays, Janice Fialka and her family selflessly offer incredibly honest stories of how they have dealt with the challenges, built the relationships, and shared their successes so others can learn and benefit. Her family is helping other families realize that, disability or not, all of us can have dreams, work hard, learn from failure, and experience sweet success.

*Beth Swedeen, Executive Director Wisconsin Board for People with Developmental Disabilities*

Janice and her family have taught me that we all thrive best in the presence of community and that we cannot expect that community to magically emerge out of nowhere. It takes organization. I have watched Janice and her family do this kind of organizing in the disability rights movement since I can remember and it has been a tremendous gift to the way I go through the world. True to form, they found a way to include each voice in their collective story. I am honored to continue to learn from Micah and his family's journey and am constantly in awe of Janice's ability to spoon from the softest places of her delicious heart and share the bounty.

*Julia Putnam, Principal, The James and Grace Lee Boggs School*

As a retired Detroit Public School teacher, Lifelong Learner and Community Educator, I am convinced that this book matters. It provides a needed framework for education that few people understand. The type of learning that combines schooling, family and community education in a substantive manner. What Matters: Reflections on Disability, Community and Love will give readers a rare education of a family's struggles, growth and willingness to be vulnerable in public about a lifestyle that few people would have the courage, understanding and love for community to share. This book will give new meaning to the word education.

*Kim Sherobbi, Detroit Public School Teacher, retired*
*James and Grace Lee Boggs Center to Nurture Community Leadership*

In this book, Janice Fialka invites us to explore and reflect upon, "What Matters". Through poetry, storytelling, and the sharing of life's struggles, she not only opens her heart to the reader, but she allows the reader's heart to open, just a bit more with each page. Her insight, her awareness, and her profound dedication will inspire you to continue to fight for justice, to live with greater compassion, and above all, to work and live from a place of love for one another, regardless of ability!

*Kristie Pretti-Frontczak, Ph.D.*

This book is a treasure. Its stories, essays, and poems guide the reader through a beautiful range of human experiences and feelings, including fear and pride, validation and inspiration, compassion and vulnerability, guilt and dignity, courage and commitment. From page to page, it walks a journey of inclusion, community, and love, inviting the reader to share in the challenges and lessons of this journey. In sharing her and her family's voyage to discover "what matters," Janice Fialka has also given us a clear and compelling way to think about the even more profound question of what it means to be a human being.

*Stephen Ward, Associate Professor, Department of Afroamerican and African Studies and the Residential College, University of Michigan*

Janice is my muse about families and disability over the lifespan— the creative source who inspires my mind, heart, and soul. I experience insight and inspiration from every interaction I have with her. I am indebted to Janice and also to her precious family--Micah, Emma, and Rich—who are her bedrock. If I could recommend a single book about family life and disability to families and professionals alike, hands down it is this one—What Matters.

*Ann P. Turnbull,*
*Distinguished Professor Emerita, Department of Special Education,*
*Co-Founder, Beach Center on Disability, University of Kansas*

***What Matters***